Old Myths and New Realities

BOOKS BY J. W. FULBRIGHT

PROSPECTS FOR THE WEST
1963

OLD MYTHS AND NEW REALITIES
AND OTHER COMMENTARIES
1964

OLD
MYTHS
AND
NEW
REALITIES

and Other Commentaries by

J. W. FULBRIGHT

CHAIRMAN
SENATE FOREIGN RELATIONS COMMITTEE
THE UNITED STATES SENATE

Random House
New York

ACKNOWLEDGMENTS

The author wishes to thank the following for permission to quote from copyright material:

Quotation on page 66 from "After the Test Ban" by Zbigniew Brzezinski, THE NEW REPUBLIC, *August 31, 1963. Copyright © 1963, Harrison-Blaine, Inc., publishers,* THE NEW REPUBLIC. ✳ *Quotation on pages 72-78 from Dr. Jerome Frank's letter to Senator Fulbright is reprinted with Dr. Frank's permission.* ✳ *Quotation on page 107 from "Partners and Allies" by Alastair Buchan,* FOREIGN AFFAIRS, *July 1963. Copyright © 1963,* FOREIGN AFFAIRS. ✳ *Quotation on page 116 from* THE UNITED STATES IN THE WORLD ARENA, *by W. W. Rostow, Harper & Brothers, 1960. Copyright © 1960, Harper & Brothers.* ✳ *Quotation on page 125 from "Arms and the Big Money Men" by Julius Duscha,* HARPER'S, *March 1964. Copyright © 1964,* HARPER'S *Magazine.* ✳ *Quotation on pages 140-141 from "Proposal for a Revolution—Part 1" by Joseph P. Lyford,* SATURDAY REVIEW, *October 19, 1963. Copyright © 1964,* SATURDAY REVIEW.

Second Printing

A5

Designed by Tere LoPrete

Foreword

These commentaries are based largely on speeches I have made, most of them within the last year. I have, however, added new material in order to expand upon ideas which necessarily were compressed when treated in speeches.

My purpose in this book is not to advance particular ideas or policy proposals, but rather to stimulate public thought and discussion free of the rigid and outdated stereotypes which stultify many of our foreign policy debates. To encourage such free-ranging discussion is one of the important responsibilities of the Congress under our Constitutional system. It is an indication of how widely this responsibility is misunderstood, by our own people as well as by foreigners, that when I made the speech on "Old Myths and New Realities," which in revised and expanded form constitutes Chapter I of this book, many persons immediately assumed that it was a "trial balloon" inspired by the White House.

It was not. My speech of March 25, 1964, as well as others on which I have drawn in preparing these commentaries, was made on my own responsibility as a Senator and without consultation with the executive branch.

It has been my custom, since becoming Chairman of the Senate Committee on Foreign Relations in 1959, to comment from time to time on the wide variety of issues that, in one form or another, come before the Committee. In so doing, I have wished neither to constrain myself, nor to put the executive branch in a possibly difficult position by associating it, through advance consultation, with my personal views. To those, at home and abroad, who may find it extraordinary that a Democratic Committee Chairman feels free to speak out without prior consultation with a Democratic President whom he admires and supports, I can only reply that I, too, see certain difficulties in the Constitutional system which gives sanction to so high a degree of independence in the legislative branch; but as long as the system remains as it is, apparently commanding the favor of the great majority of the American people, I shall continue, with my colleagues, to try to meet my responsibilities in the manner prescribed by American Constitutional practice.

A vital distinction must be made between offering broad policy directions, and interfering in the conduct of policy by the executive branch. Many of our difficulties in foreign policy arise, not only from our addiction to old myths in the face of new realities, but also from a recurring tendency on the part of Congress to overstep its proper role. Our history is strewn with examples, which have invariably had unhappy results, of Congressional efforts to exercise executive functions. The agitation of the "war hawks" of 1812, and of the Committee on the Conduct of the War in the 1860s, and the neutrality legislation of the 1930s are among the more striking instances which may be cited from the past of the Congress either forcing or binding the hands of the executive. In recent years, this tendency on the part of Congress has been most evident with respect to the foreign aid program; but it is also observable in the network of legislative restrictions inhibiting our actions relative to nations in the Communist bloc.

Discussion of the role of Congress in foreign policy, especially in brief and general terms, as is necessarily the case here, is always likely to subject one to the charge that he seeks to reduce Congress to a rubber stamp or to give the executive a blank check. This accusation misses the point and leads to a sterile argument.

Congress, and especially the Senate, does have a role in foreign policy. This role is to participate in shaping broad policies which, if they are to be viable, must reflect a national consensus. It is a proper exercise of this role for the Congress to determine, for example, whether there should be a foreign aid program. But if this determination is in the affirmative, the executive should then be left free, within broadly defined limits of scope and direction, to carry out the program and to adapt it to the constantly changing conditions with which we are confronted throughout the world. I am not arguing the Constitutional right or power of Congress to hem in the program with page after page of restrictions; I am only challenging the wisdom of such a course.

Still less am I arguing a doctrine of executive infallibility. There can be no guarantee that human beings, in either the White House or the Capitol, will not make mistakes or do foolish things. But these mistakes are more likely to be quickly and easily correctable if they are errors of executive judgment than if they are the result of directives embedded and sanctified in legislation.

It is also a proper and important part of the Congressional role in foreign policy to take the lead in what ought to be a continuing national discussion and examination of the posture of the United States in the world, of our basic national interests, and of ways and means of advancing those interests. It is out of such discussion that we arrive gradually at a broad national consensus which not only gives direction to our policies, but also provides the essential base of public support the executive needs to carry out those policies from day to day and week to week.

It is in an effort to stimulate such discussion and to contribute to it that I have prepared this small book; it was in such an effort that I made the speeches upon which the book draws. If this effort leads to a dispassionate consideration of some "unthinkable thoughts"—even if those thoughts are rejected upon mature reflection—my purpose will have been amply served.

J. W. FULBRIGHT

Washington, D.C./May, 1964

Contents

Old Myths and New Realities

I

Old Myths and New Realities

There is an inevitable divergence, attributable to the imperfections of the human mind, between the world as it is and the world as men perceive it. As long as our perceptions are reasonably close to objective reality, it is possible for us to act upon our problems in a rational and appropriate manner. But when our perceptions fail to keep pace with events, when we refuse to believe something because it displeases or frightens us, or is simply startlingly unfamiliar, then the gap between fact and perception becomes a chasm, and action becomes irrelevant and irrational.

(3)

There has always—and inevitably—been some divergence between the realities of foreign policy and our ideas about it. This divergence has in certain respects been growing rather than narrowing, and we are handicapped, accordingly, by policies based on old myths rather than current realities. The divergence is dangerous and unnecessary— dangerous because it can reduce foreign policy to a fraudulent game of imagery and appearances, unnecessary because it can be overcome by the determination of men in high office to dispel prevailing misconceptions through the candid dissemination of unpleasant but inescapable facts.

Before commenting on some of the specific areas where I believe our policies are at least partially based on cherished myths rather than objective facts, I should like to suggest two possible reasons for the growing divergence between the realities and our perceptions of current world politics. The first is the radical change in relations between and within the Communist and the free worlds, and the second is the tendency of too many of us to confuse means with ends and, accordingly, to adhere to prevailing practices with a fervor befitting immutable principles.

Although it is too soon to render a definitive judgment, there is mounting evidence that events of recent years have wrought profound changes in the character of East-West relations. In the Cuban

(4)

missile crisis of October, 1962, the United States proved to the Soviet Union that a policy of aggression and adventure involved unacceptable risks. In the signing of the test ban treaty each side in effect assured the other that it was prepared to forego, at least for the present, any bid for a decisive military or political breakthrough. These occurrences, it should be added, took place against the background of the clearly understood strategic superiority of the United States.

It seems reasonable, therefore, to suggest that the character of the cold war has, for the present at least, been profoundly altered: by the drawing back of the Soviet Union from extremely aggressive policies; by the implicit repudiation, by both sides, of a policy of "total victory"; and by the establishment of an American strategic superiority which the Soviet Union appears to have tacitly accepted because it has been accompanied by assurances that it will be exercised by the United States with responsibility and restraint. These enormously important changes may come to be regarded by historians as the foremost achievements of the Kennedy Administration in the field of foreign policy. Their effect has been to commit us to a foreign policy which can accurately—though perhaps not prudently—be defined as one of "peaceful coexistence."

Another of the results of the lowering of ten-

sions between East and West is that each is now
free to enjoy the luxury of accelerated strife and
squabbling within its own domain. The ideological
thunderbolts between Washington and Moscow,
which until a few years ago seemed a permanent
part of our daily lives, have become pale shadows
of their former selves. Now instead the United
States waits in fascinated apprehension for the
Olympian pronouncements that issue from Paris
at six-month intervals, while the Russians respond
to the crude epithets of Peking with almost plain-
tive rejoinders about "those who want to start a
war against everybody."

These astonishing changes in the configuration
of the postwar world have had an unsettling effect
on both public and official opinion in the United
States. One reason for this, I believe, lies in the
fact that we are a people used to looking at the
world, and indeed at ourselves, in moralistic rather
than empirical terms. We are predisposed to regard any conflict as a clash between good and evil
rather than as simply a clash between conflicting
interests. We are inclined to confuse freedom and
democracy, which we regard as moral principles,
with the way in which they are practiced in America—with capitalism, federalism, and the two-
party system, which are not moral principles but
simply the preferred and accepted practices of the
American people. There is much cant in American

moralism and not a little inconsistency. It resembles in some ways the religious faith of the many respectable people who, in Samuel Butler's words, "would be equally horrified to hear the Christian religion doubted or to see it practiced."

Our national vocabulary is full of "self-evident truths," not only about "life, liberty, and happiness," but about a vast number of personal and public issues, including the cold war. It has become one of the "self-evident truths" of the postwar era that, just as the President resides in Washington and the Pope in Rome, the Devil resides immutably in Moscow. We have come to regard the Kremlin as the permanent seat of his power and we have grown almost comfortable with a menace which, though unspeakably evil, has had the redeeming virtues of constancy, predictability, and familiarity. Now the Devil has betrayed us by traveling abroad and, worse still, by dispersing himself, turning up now here, now there, and in many places at once, with a devilish disregard for the laboriously constructed frontiers of ideology.

We are confronted with a complex and fluid world situation, and we are not adapting ourselves to it. We are clinging to old myths in the face of new realities, and we are seeking to escape the contradictions by narrowing the permissible bounds of public discussion, by relegating an increasing number of ideas and viewpoints to a growing cate-

gory of "unthinkable thoughts." I believe that this
tendency can and should be reversed, that it is
within our ability, and unquestionably in our interests, to cut loose from established myths and to
start thinking some "unthinkable thoughts"—about
the cold war and East-West relations, about the
underdeveloped countries and particularly those
in Latin America, about the changing nature of
the Chinese Communist threat in Asia, and about
the festering war in Vietnam.

The master myth of the cold war is that the
Communist bloc is a monolith composed of governments which are not really governments at all,
but organized conspiracies, divided among themselves perhaps in certain matters of tactics, but all
equally resolute and implacable in their determination to destroy the free world.

I believe that the Communist world is indeed
hostile to the free world in its general and long-
term intentions, but that the existence of this ani-
mosity in principle is far less important for our
foreign policy than the great variations in its in-
tensity and character both in time and among the
individual members of the Communist bloc. Only
if we recognize these variations, ranging from
China, which poses immediate threats to the free
world, to Poland and Yugoslavia, which pose none,
can we hope to act effectively upon the bloc and

to turn its internal differences to our own advantage and to the advantage of those bloc countries which wish to maximize their independence. It is the responsibility of our national leaders, both in the executive branch and in Congress, to acknowledge and act upon these realities, even at the cost of saying things which will not win immediate widespread enthusiasm.

For a start, we can acknowledge the fact that the Soviet Union, though still a most formidable adversary, has ceased to be totally and implacably hostile to the West. It has shown a new willingness to enter mutually advantageous arrangements with the West and, thus far at least, to honor them. It has therefore become possible to divert some of our energies from the prosecution of the cold war to the relaxation of the cold war and to deal with the Soviet Union, for certain purposes, as a normal state with normal and traditional interests.

If we are to do these things effectively, we must distinguish between communism as an ideology and the power and policy of the Soviet state. It is not communism as a doctrine, or communism as it is practiced *within* the Soviet Union or *within* any other country, that threatens us. How the Soviet Union organizes its internal life, the gods and doctrines that it worships, are matters for the Soviet Union to determine. It is not Communist dogma as espoused within Russia but Communist imperialism that threatens us and other peoples of the non-Communist world. Insofar as a great nation mobilizes its power and resources for aggressive purposes, that nation, regardless of ideology, makes itself our enemy. Insofar as a nation is content to practice its doctrines within its own frontiers, that nation—except under certain extreme circumstances—is one with which we have no proper quarrel. We must deal with the Soviet Union as a great power, quite apart from differences of ideology. To the extent that the Soviet leaders abandon the global ambitions of Marxist ideology, in fact if not in words, it becomes possible for us to engage in normal relations with them, relations which probably cannot be close or trusting for many years to come but which can be gradually freed of the terror and the tensions of the cold war.

In our relations with the Russians, and indeed in our relations with all nations, we would do well to remember, and to act upon, the words of Pope John in the great Encyclical *Pacem in Terris*: "It must be borne in mind," said Pope John, "that to proceed gradually is the law of life in all its expressions; therefore, in human institutions, too, it is not possible to renovate for the better except by working from within them, gradually . . . Violence has always achieved only destruction, not construction, the kindling of passions, not their pacification, the accumulation of hate and ruin, not the reconciliation of the contending parties. And it has reduced men and parties to the difficult task of rebuilding, after sad experience, on the ruins of discord. . . ."

Important opportunities have been created for Western policy by the development of "polycentrism" in the Communist bloc. The Communist nations, as George Kennan has pointed out, are, like the Western nations, currently caught up in a crisis of indecision about their relations with countries outside their own ideological bloc. The choices open to the satellite states are limited but by no means insignificant. They can adhere slavishly to Soviet preferences or they can strike out on their own, within limits, to enter into mutually advantageous relations with the West.

Whether they do so, and to what extent, is to some degree within the power of the West to determine. If we persist in the view that all Communist regimes are equally hostile and equally threatening to the West, and that we can have no policy toward the "captive nations" except the eventual overthrow of their Communist regimes, then the West may enforce upon the Communist bloc a degree of unity which the Soviet Union has shown itself to be quite incapable of imposing— just as Stalin in the early postwar years frightened the West into a degree of unity that it almost certainly could not have attained by its own unaided efforts. If, on the other hand, we are willing to re-examine the view that all Communist regimes are alike in the threat which they pose for the West—a view which had a certain validity in Stalin's time—then we may be able to exert an important influence on the course of events within a divided Communist world.

We are to a great extent the victims, and the Soviets the beneficiaries, of our own ideological convictions and of the curious contradictions which they involve. We consider it a form of subversion of the free world, for example, when the Russians enter trade relations or conclude a consular convention or establish airline connections with a free country in Asia, Africa, or Latin America—and to a certain extent we are right. On the other hand, when it is proposed that we adopt the same strategy in reverse—by extending commercial credits to Poland or Yugoslavia, or by exchanging ambassadors with a Hungarian regime which has changed considerably in character since the revolution of 1956—then the same patriots who are so alarmed by Soviet activities in the free world charge our policy-makers with "giving aid and comfort to the enemy," and with innumerable other categories of idiocy and immorality.

It is time that we resolved this contradiction and separated myth from reality. The myth is that every Communist state is an unmitigated evil and a relentless enemy of the free world; the reality is that some Communist regimes pose a threat to the free world while others pose little or none, and that if we will recognize these distinctions, we ourselves will be able to influence events in the Communist bloc in a way favorable to the security of the free world. "It could well be argued," writes George Kennan, ". . . that if the major Western powers had full freedom of movement in devising their own policies, it would be within their power to determine whether the Chinese view, or the Soviet view, or perhaps a view more liberal than either would ultimately prevail within the Communist camp."[1]

There are numerous areas in which we can seek to reduce the tensions of the cold war and to bring a degree of normalcy into our relations with the Soviet Union and other Communist countries— once we have resolved that it is safe and wise to do so. We have already taken important steps in this direction: the Antarctic and Austrian treaties and the nuclear test ban treaty, the broadening of East-West cultural and educational relations, and the expansion of trade.

On the basis of recent experience and present economic needs, there seems little likelihood of a

[1] George Kennan, "Polycentrism and Western Policy," *Foreign Affairs,* January, 1964, p. 178.

spectacular increase in trade between Communist and Western countries, even if existing restrictions were to be relaxed. Free-world trade with Communist countries has been increasing at a steady but unspectacular rate, and it seems unlikely to be greatly accelerated because of the limited ability of the Communist countries to pay for increased imports. A modest increase in East-West trade may nonetheless serve as a modest instrument of East-West *détente*—provided that we are able to overcome the myth that trade with Communist countries is a compact with the Devil, and to recognize that, on the contrary, trade in nonstrategic goods can serve as an effective and honorable means of advancing both peace and human welfare.

Whether we are able to make these philosophic adjustments or not, we cannot escape the fact that our allies are going to trade with the Communist bloc whether we like it or not. The world's major exporting nations are slowly but steadily increasing their trade with the Communist bloc, and the bloc countries are showing themselves to be reliable customers. Since 1958 Western Europe has been increasing its exports to the East at the rate of about 7 percent a year, which is nearly the same rate at which its overall world sales have been increasing.

West Germany is by far the leading Western nation in trade with the Sino-Soviet bloc. West

German exports to bloc countries in 1962 were valued at $749.9 million. Britain was in second place—although not a close second—with exports to Communist countries amounting to $393 million in 1962. France followed with exports worth $313.4 million, and the figure for the United States —consisting largely of surplus food sales to Poland under Public Law 480—stood far below at $125.1 million.

Our allies have made it plain that they propose to expand this trade in nonstrategic goods wherever possible. West Germany, since the fall of 1962, has exchanged or agreed to exchange trade missions with every country in Eastern Europe except Albania. Britain has indicated that she will soon extend long-term credits to Communist countries, breaching the five-year limit which the Western Allies have hitherto observed. In the light of these facts, it is difficult to see what effect the tight American trade policies have other than to deny the United States a substantial share of a profitable market.

The inability of the United States to prevent its partners from trading extensively with the Communist bloc is one good reason for relaxing our own restrictions, but there is a better reason: the potential value of trade—a moderate volume of trade in nonstrategic items—as an instrument for reducing world tensions and strengthening the foundations of peace. I do not think that trade or the nuclear test ban, or any other prospective East-West accommodation, will lead to a grand reconciliation that will end the cold war and usher in the brotherhood of man. At most, the cumulative effect of all the agreements that are likely to be attainable in the foreseeable future will be the alleviation of the extreme tensions and animosities that threaten the world with nuclear devastation, and the gradual conversion of the struggle between communism and the free world into a safer and more tolerable international rivalry, one which may be with us for years and decades to come but which need not be so terrifying and so costly as to distract the nations of the world from the creative pursuits of civilized societies.

There is little in history to justify the expectation that we can either win the cold war or end it immediately and completely. These are favored myths, respectively, of the American right and of the American left. They are, I believe, equal in their unreality and in their disregard for the feasibilities of history. We must disabuse ourselves of them and come to terms, at last, with the realities of a world in which neither good nor evil is absolute and in which those who move events and make history are those who have understood not how much but how little it is within our power to change.

Latin America is one of the areas of the world in which American policy is weakened by a growing divergency between old myths and new realities.

The crisis of early 1964 over the Panama Canal was unnecessarily protracted for reasons of domestic politics and national pride and sensitivity on both sides—for reasons, that is, of only marginal relevance to the merits of the dispute. I think the Panamanians have unquestionably been more emotional about the dispute than has the United States. I also think that there is less reason for emotionalism on the part of the United States than on the part of Panama. It is important for us to remember that the issue over the Canal, temporarily abated but not resolved by the preliminary agreement of April 3, 1964, is only one of a great many in which the United States is involved, and by no means the most important. For Panama, on the other hand, a small nation with a weak economy and an uncertain government, the Canal is the pre-eminent factor in the nation's economy and in its foreign relations. Surely, in a confrontation so unequal, it is not unreasonable to expect the United States to go a little further than halfway in the search for a fair settlement.

Under the accord of April 3, 1964, Panama and the United States agreed to designate special ambassadors to "seek the prompt elimination of the causes of conflict between the two countries." This reasonable and statesmanlike resolution of the immediate crisis was achieved only after a protracted debate over whether the status of the Canal under the treaty of 1903 was to be "discussed" or "negotiated." This debate had much more to do with the national pride and sensitivity of both countries than with the substance of the dispute itself. As we proceed to "review" or "discuss" or "negotiate" the status of the Canal and, more importantly, of the Canal Zone, it is to be hoped that we will avoid extraneous matters and focus our negotiating efforts on the two basic realities of the situation: the need of the United States and other maritime powers for a secure and adequate water route across the Central American isthmus; and the need of Panama, in this era of rising nationalism in Latin America, for an instrument more compatible with her psychological needs than the treaty of 1903.

We Americans would do well to divest ourselves of the silly notion that the issue with Panama is a test of our courage and resolve. I believe that the Cuban missile crisis of 1962, involving a confrontation with nuclear weapons and intercontinental missiles, was indeed a test of our courage, and we acquitted ourselves extremely well. I am unable to understand how a controversy with a small and poor country, with virtually no military capacity, can possibly be regarded as a test of our bravery and will to defend our interests. It takes stubbornness but not courage to reject the entreaties of the weak. The real test in Panama is not of our valor but of our wisdom and judgment and common sense.

We would also do well to disabuse ourselves of the myth that there is something morally sacred about the treaty of 1903. The fact of the matter is that the treaty was concluded under circumstances that reflect little credit on the United States. It was made possible by Panama's separation from Colombia, which probably could not have occurred at that time without the dispatch of United States warships to prevent the landing of Colombian troops on the isthmus to put down the Panamanian rebellion. The United States not only intervened in Colombia's internal affairs, but did so in violation of a treaty concluded in 1846 under which the United States had *guaranteed* Colombian sovereignty over the isthmus. President Theodore Roosevelt, as he boasted, "took Panama," and proceeded to negotiate the Canal treaty with a compliant Panamanian regime. Panamanians contend that they were "shotgunned" into the treaty of 1903 as the price of United States protection against a possible effort by Colombia to recover the isthmus. The contention is not without substance.

It is not my purpose here to relate the events

of sixty years ago, but only to suggest that there is little basis for a posture of injured innocence and self-righteousness by either side and that we would do much better to resolve the issue on the basis of present realities rather than old myths.

The central reality is that the treaty of 1903 is in certain respects obsolete. The treaty has been revised only twice, in 1936 when the annual rental was raised from $250,000 to $430,000 and other modifications were made, and in 1955 when further changes were made, including an increase in the annual rental to $1.9 million, where it now stands. The Canal of course contributes far more to the Panamanian economy in the form of wages paid to Panamanian workers and purchases made in Panama. The fact remains, nonetheless, that the annual rental of $1.9 million is a modest sum and should be increased. There are other issues, relating to hiring policies for Panamanian workers in the Zone, the flying of flags, and other symbols of national pride and sovereignty. The basic problem about the treaty, however, is the exercise of American control over a part of the territory of Panama in this age of intense nationalist and anticolonialist feeling. Justly or not, the Panamanians feel that they are being treated as a colony, or a quasi-colony, of the United States, and this feeling is accentuated by the contrast between the standard of living of the Panamanians, with a per capita income of about $429 a year, and that of the Americans living in the Canal Zone, with a per capita income of $4,228 a year. It is the profound social and economic alienation between Panama and the Canal Zone, and its impact on the national feeling of the Panamanians, that underlies the periodic crises that arise over the Canal.

Under these circumstances, it seems to me entirely proper and necessary for the United States to take the initiative in proposing new arrangements that would redress some of Panama's grievances against the treaty as it now stands. I see no reason—certainly no reason of "weakness" or "dishonor"—why the United States cannot commit itself positively and clearly to negotiate revisions in the Canal treaty, and to submit such changes as are made to the Senate for its advice and consent.

In the long run, the growing volume of interoceanic traffic and the increased size of such vessels as oil tankers and aircraft carriers will require the construction of a larger, sea-level canal. At such time as plans for a new sea-level canal are formulated, it seems to me that we should consider the possibility of its being constructed and operated by an international consortium rather than by the United States alone. Such a consortium might consist of the principal users of the present Panama Canal, with each user's contribution to the construction of the new canal and voting power in the corporation that would govern it to be determined by a formula reflecting the volume of the particular user's traffic through the old canal and the prospective volume of its traffic through the new canal. The host country would be given a special position in the governing body of the new canal, and a special position might also be found for the Organization of American States as representative of the hemisphere.

The advantages of a consortium for the United States are considerable. It would save us substantial expenditures in the building of the canal and, what is more important, it would spare us the extremely sensitive political problems connected with being the sole proprietor of an international thoroughfare across the territory of another country. As the British learned at Suez and as we have now learned in Panama, there are few rewards and enormous difficulties involved in the exercise of special responsibilities within the borders of a small country where nationalism is a strong and rising force.

The Soviet Union is of course one of the users of the Panama Canal, albeit a minor one, and this fact suggests an "unthinkable thought": the possibility of Soviet participation in a consortium constituted to build and operate a new Central American canal. I am not advocating Soviet participation, but neither do I think it must be ruled out as "unthinkable."

The first question that comes to mind is whether the Russians, as members of the consortium, would be in a position to disrupt the operation of a new canal. Certainly under a reasonable consortium agreement no single member would have the authority to close the canal or disrupt the flow of traffic, and none would have any armed strength in the area of the canal, except perhaps for individual members of a zonal police force. Nor, being a sea-level waterway, would the canal have locks or other complex machinery which might be damaged by sabotage. If the consortium were formed under these conditions, how would the Russians be able to use their membership to disrupt the operation of the canal even if they wanted to?

It may of course be argued that Soviet participation in a canal consortium would give them a base for subversion in Latin America, but it is difficult to see what significant opportunities for subversive activities would be provided that are not already fully available through other channels.

A more important question is whether Soviet participation in a canal consortium would be of positive benefit to the United States, and if so, how. First of all, it would obligate them to contribute to the costs of building the canal, and who would find this prospect objectionable in itself?

And more fundamental questions present themselves: Would not Soviet participation in a canal consortium tend to strengthen their commitment to a peaceful status quo, just as their adherence to the Antarctic Treaty has made them co-operative associates in keeping the cold war away from the Antarctic continent? Is there not something to be gained for world peace and stability from an arrangement which would bring the Russians into close co-operation with nations they regard as "imperialists" in a kind of enterprise which they have hitherto denounced as "imperialist exploitation"? Would there not be significant psychological symbolism in the Soviet Union sharing responsibility for the construction and maintenance of a vital international facility, if only because of the striking contrast with the more disruptive activities of their revolutionary past? In summary, is there not something to be gained for world peace from bringing a difficult and dangerous nation into one more enterprise in which co-operation in the performance of practical tasks would be permitted to do its eroding work on the ideological passions that divide us?

The problem of Cuba is more difficult than that of Panama, and far more heavily burdened with the dead weight of old myths and prohibitions against "unthinkable thoughts." I think the time is overdue for a candid re-evaluation of our Cuban policy even though it may lead to distasteful conclusions.

I begin with the premise that the continued existence of the Castro regime in Cuba is inimical to the interests of the United States, and that these interests would be far better served by a Cuban government oriented toward liberal democracy. The problem for American policy, however, is not in defining what we would like; it is, rather, how to achieve what we would like or, failing that, how to live with the best that we can get.

Specifically, in the case of Cuba, the problem is one of balancing ends and means, of putting—and keeping—the difficulties posed by that unhappy island in proper perspective. It is clear that the existence of the Castro regime is inimical to our interests. The real question is, how inimical? Enough to justify an invasion by United States armed forces? enough to justify a naval blockade? or an economic boycott? or support, either open or secret, for anti-Castro Cubans?

One cannot be dogmatic in answering these questions, because the answers vary from one time to another, depending not upon the ideology but upon the actions of the Castro Government, and and upon those of its patrons in Moscow. Thus, for example, when the Soviets installed medium-range ballistic missiles in Cuba, the threat to the United

States was sufficient to warrant a selective blockade, and *if* this had not achieved our purpose, we
were quite prepared—and justifiably so—to invade
the island. With no offensive weapons in Cuba, the
threat is less, and the measures appropriate to deal
with it are reduced correspondingly.

One of the inhibitions to a realistic approach to
the problem of Cuba is the myth that we are still
in the era when, as Secretary of State Richard
Olney put it in 1895, "the United States is practi-
cally sovereign on this continent, and its fiat is law
upon those subjects to which it confines its inter-
position." This might have been so in 1895 (though
even that can be argued), but it is clearly not so
in 1964. The trouble is that a great many people
apparently wish it were so, and persist in demand-
ing that the United States Government act as if
it were. The near-hysteria that has afflicted many
Americans over Cuba comes more from wounded
pride than from anything else. We are told that
the Castro regime is "intolerable," despite the plain
fact that, rightly or wrongly, we have tolerated it
for more than five years.

If we look at Cuba rationally instead of emotionally, if we shed our nostalgia and frustrations, we
see an island of 6 million people led by an erratic
demagogue who is not only communizing his own
country but who is also doing his best to subvert
much of the rest of Latin America. Therein lies the

threat of Castro, not to the United States but, in varying degrees, to other countries of Latin America. And the source of the threat lies more in Moscow than in Havana, which, on its own, would lack the resources to do very much.

Broadly speaking, there are two ways to deal with this threat: The first possibility is the forcible overthrow of the Castro Government, which would deprive the Soviet Union of its most important base in the Western Hemisphere—although not its only base (Soviet Embassies in Mexico City and Montevideo, for example, are important centers of propaganda and similar activities). The overthrow of Castro might be accomplished, in theory at least, either from within or without, either directly or indirectly. The second approach is the isolation of the Castro regime, combined with efforts to insulate and strengthen the rest of Latin America against its subversive efforts.

These options, of course, are not mutually exclusive: a policy designed to isolate Castro might also contribute to his overthrow. But neither the overthrow of the Castro regime nor its complete isolation would solve the problems of the United States in Latin America. These problems are aggravated by Castro, but they are not caused by him. They are the result of a process of rapid and profound change in societies which are stubbornly resistant to change. If Cuba were to sink below the

Caribbean tomorrow, and if Moscow were suddenly and miraculously to recall all of its agents in the Western Hemisphere, much of Latin America would still be agitated by unrest, radicalism, and revolution.

Nonetheless, the disappearance of Castro would assuredly make those problems easier to solve. It is apparent, however, that this is not going to come about except through the use of means which are wholly disproportionate to the objective. The fact that we do not like Castro is hardly sufficient grounds to go to war against him.

Except for the abortive effort at the Bay of Pigs, the United States has generally followed the second of my suggested alternatives—a policy, that is, of isolating Cuba and of strengthening the Hemisphere against its subversive activities. I approve of this policy. But in applying it, we have to weigh costs in terms of results. We have to ask ourselves, for example, whether it is worth disrupting Anglo-American relations in an effort, so far unsuccessful, to persuade our British friends not to sell buses to Cuba or to take steps to keep their ships out of the Cuba trade. If we cannot persuade them, after a reasonable presentation of our case, to follow our recommendations, it is questionable whether it is worth-while to make a major issue of the matter. This is especially so inasmuch as our policy of economic denial is cal-

culated to restrain Cuba, to make life more difficult
for Castro, and to make him a more expensive ally
for the Soviet Union, but not to overthrow him.

In cutting off military assistance to Great Britain, France, and Yugoslavia, as it did on February 18, 1964, in retaliation for their failure to
remove their shipping from the Cuba trade, the
United States wielded a stuffed club. The amounts
of aid involved were infinitesimal; the chances of
gaining compliance with our boycott policy were
nil; and the annoyance of the countries concerned
was considerable. What we terminated with respect to Britain and France, in fact, can hardly be
called aid; it was a sales promotion program under
which British and French military leaders were
brought to the United States to see—and to buy—
advanced American weapons. Terminating this
program was in itself of little importance; Britain
and France do not need our assistance. But terminating the program as a sanction against their trade
with Cuba can have no real effect other than to
create an illusory image of "toughness" for the
benefit of our own people.

I should like to make it very clear that I am not
arguing against the desirability of a concerted
free-world economic boycott against the Castro
regime, but against its feasibility. The effort has
been made, and all the fulminations we can utter
about sanctions and retaliation against free-world

countries that trade with Cuba cannot long conceal the fact that the boycott policy is a failure as an instrument for bringing about the fall of the Castro regime.

I believe that the United States under present conditions should maintain its *own* political and economic boycott of the Castro regime. Communist Cuba is hostile to the United States and poses a continuing threat of subversion in Latin America. As long as this remains true, it is clearly not in our interests to do anything that would help the Castro regime to sustain itself.

The boycott policy—or, more precisely, the policy of seeking to bring about the fall of the Castro regime through a concerted free-world boycott—has not failed because of any "weakness" or "timidity" on the part of our government. This charge, so frequently heard, is one of the most pernicious myths to have been inflicted on the American people. The boycott policy has failed because the United States is not omnipotent and cannot be. The basic reality to be faced is that it is simply not within our power to compel our allies to cut off their trade with Cuba, unless we are prepared to take drastic sanctions against them, such as closing our own markets to any foreign company that does business in Cuba. We can do this of course, but if we do, we ought first to be very sure that the Cuban boycott is more important to us than good relations with our closest allies. In fact, even the most drastic sanctions are as likely to be rewarded with defiance as with compliance. For practical purposes, all we can do is *ask* other countries to take the measures with respect to Cuba which we recommend. We have done so, and in some areas have been successful. In other areas, notably that of the economic boycott, we have asked for the full co-operation of other free-world countries, and it has been largely denied. It remains for us to decide whether we will respond with a sustained outburst of hollow and ill-tempered threats, all the while comforting ourselves with the myth that we can get anything we want if only we try hard enough—or, in this case, shout loud enough—or we can acknowledge the failure of our efforts and proceed, coolly and rationally, to re-examine the policies which we now pursue in relation to the interests they are intended to serve.

The prospects of bringing down the Castro regime by political and economic boycott have never been very good. Even if a general free-world boycott were successfully applied against Cuba, it is unlikely that the Russians would refuse to carry the extra financial burden, and thereby permit the only Communist regime in the Western Hemisphere to collapse. We are thus compelled to recognize that there is probably no way of bringing down the Castro regime by means of economic pressures unless we are prepared to impose a blockade against *nonmilitary* shipments from the Soviet Union. Exactly such a policy has been recommended by some of our more reckless politicians, but the preponderance of informed opinion is that a blockade against Soviet shipments of *nonmilitary* supplies to Cuba would be extravagantly dangerous, carrying the strong possibility of a confrontation that could explode into nuclear war.

It seems to me that we are left, then, with the acceptance of the continued existence of the Castro regime as a distasteful nuisance but not an intolerable danger so long as the nations of the Hemisphere are prepared to meet their obligations of collective defense under the Rio Treaty.

In recent years we have become transfixed with Cuba, making it far more important in both our foreign relations and in our domestic life than its size and influence warrant. We have flattered a noisy but minor demagogue by treating him as if he were a Napoleonic menace. Communist Cuba has been a disruptive and subversive influence in Venezuela and other countries of the Hemisphere, and there is no doubt that both we and our Latin American partners would be better off if the Castro regime did not exist. But it is important to bear

(3 2)

in mind that, despite their best efforts, the Cuban Communists have not succeeded in subverting the Hemisphere, and that in Venezuela, for example, where communism has made a major effort to gain power through terrorism, it has been repudiated in a free election by a people who have committed themselves to the course of liberal democracy. It is necessary to weigh the desirability of an objective against the feasibility of its attainment, and when we do this with respect to Cuba, I think we are bound to conclude that Castro is a nuisance but not a grave threat to the United States and that he cannot be gotten rid of except by means that are wholly disproportionate to the objective. Cuban communism does pose a grave threat to other Latin American countries, but this threat can be dealt with by prompt and vigorous use of the established procedures of the inter-American system against any act of aggression.

To a considerable extent, these procedures have already been put to effective use. The Organization of American States has found the Castro regime to be incompatible with the principles of the inter-American system, and Cuba has been excluded from the inter-American organization. Fifteen of the Latin American states have broken diplomatic relations with Cuba. There has been increasing inter-American co-operation in the exchange of

(*33*)

intelligence and in the application of countersub-
versive measures. Latin American trade with Cuba
is insignificant.

Nonetheless, Cuban intervention in the affairs
of Latin American states has continued, the most
flagrant example being the shipment of arms to
Venezuela, a shipment which was fully confirmed
and documented by a committee of the Organization of American States. The Organization of
American States is the deliberately chosen instrument of the American states to deal with such
problems. It has available to it adequate procedures and powers, based in the Rio Treaty and the
Charter of the Organization of American States.
The United States, of course, must meet its obligations under these treaties by participating fully,
and indeed leading, in collective action against
aggression and subversion. But the defense of
Latin America is ultimately a Latin American
responsibility; however much we may wish to do
so, we cannot protect people who are not interested
in protecting themselves. If, on the other hand, the
Latin American republics join with us in the
effective use of the Organization of American
States to counter Cuban intervention in other
countries, it is possible that the Castro regime will
come to see the high price and futility of subversion, and will cease its interference in the Hemisphere.

In summary, I think that we must abandon the myth that Cuban communism is a transitory menace and face up to two basic realities about Cuba: first, that the Castro regime is not on the verge of collapse and is not likely to be overthrown by any policies which we are now pursuing or can reasonably undertake; and second, that the continued existence of the Castro regime, though inimical to our interests and policies, is not an insuperable obstacle to the attainment of our objectives, unless we make it so by permitting it to poison our politics at home and to divert us from more important tasks in the Hemisphere.

The policy of the United States with respect to Latin America as a whole is predicated on the assumption that social revolution can be accomplished without violent upheaval. This is the guiding principle of the Alliance for Progress and it may in time be vindicated. We are entitled to hope so, and it is wise and necessary for us to do all that we can to advance the prospects of peaceful and orderly reform.

At the same time, we must be under no illusions as to the extreme difficulty of uprooting long-established ruling oligarchies without disruptions involving lesser or greater degrees of violence. The historical odds are probably against the prospects of peaceful social revolution. There are places, of course, where it has occurred, and others where it seems likely to occur. In Latin America, the chances for such basic change by peaceful means seem bright in Colombia and Venezuela and certain other countries; in Mexico many basic changes have been made by peaceful means, but these came in the wake of a violent revolution. In some other Latin American countries the power of ruling oligarchies is so solidly established and their ignorance so great that the forceful overthrow of established authorities may be unavoidable.

I am not predicting violent revolutions in Latin America or elsewhere. Still less am I advocating them. I wish only to suggest that violent social revolutions are a possibility in countries where feudal oligarchies resist all meaningful change by peaceful means. We must not, in our preference for the democratic procedures envisioned by the Charter of Punta del Este, close our minds to the possibility that democratic procedures may fail in certain countries, and that where democracy does fail violent social convulsions may occur.

We would do well, while continuing our efforts to promote peaceful change through the Alliance for Progress, to consider what our reactions might be in the event of the outbreak of genuine social revolution in one or more Latin American countries. Such a revolution did occur in Bolivia, and we accepted it calmly and sensibly. But what if a violent social revolution were to break out in one of the larger Latin American countries? Would we feel certain that it was Cuban or Soviet inspired? Would we wish to intervene on the side of established authority? Or would we be willing to tolerate or even support a revolution if it was seen to be not Communist but similar in nature to the Mexican revolution or the Nasser revolution in Egpyt?

These are hypothetical questions and there is no readily available set of answers to them. But they are questions which we should be thinking about because they have to do with problems that could become real and urgent with great suddenness. We would be considering, for example, what groups in particular countries might conceivably lead revolutionary movements, and if we can identify them, we should be considering how we might communicate with them and influence them in such a way that their movements, if successful, will not pursue courses detrimental to our security and our interests.

The Far East is another area of the world in which American policy is handicapped by the divergence of old myths and new realities. Particularly with respect to China, an elaborate vocabulary of make-believe has become compulsory in both official and public discussion. We are committed, with respect to China and other areas in Asia, to inflexible policies of long standing from which we hesitate to depart because of the attribution to these policies of an aura of mystical sanctity. It may be that a thorough re-evaluation of our Far Eastern policies would lead us to the conclusion that they are sound and wise, or at least that they represent the best available options. It may be, on the other hand, that a re-evaluation would point up the need for greater or lesser changes in our policies. The point is that whatever the outcome of a re-thinking of policy might be, we have been unwilling to undertake it because of the fear of many government officials, undoubtedly well founded, that even the suggestion of new policies toward China would provoke a vehement public outcry.

I do not think that the United States can or should recognize Communist China or acquiesce in her admission to the United Nations under present circumstances. It would be unwise to do so because there is nothing to be gained by it so long as the Peking regime maintains its attitude of implacable hostility toward the United States. Furthermore, recognition, which has been withheld since 1949, could hardly be interpreted at present as the simple acknowledgment of a fact. Unless it were accompanied by altered policies on the part of Communist China, recognition would have the distinct appearance of *approval,* not because it ought to—indeed, it should not—but because, having withheld recognition for fifteen years as a sign of our disapproval, we could hardly accord it now without having it take on an opposite meaning, although that is neither intended nor desired. The conclusion to which this leads us, beyond the inadvisability of recognizing Communist China at present, is the unwisdom and self-defeating consequences of attributing moral significance to the recognition of governments, or, indeed, of using it for any purpose other than the acknowledgement of existing facts.

I do not believe, however, that the present state of affairs with respect to China is necessarily permanent. As we have seen in our relations with Germany and Japan, hostility can give way in an astonishingly short time to close friendship; and as we have seen in our relations with China, the reverse can occur with equal speed. It is not impossible that in time our relations with China will change again, if not to friendship then perhaps to "competitive coexistence." It would therefore be an extremely useful thing if we could introduce an element of flexibility, or, more precisely, of the capacity to be flexible, into our relations with Communist China.

We would do well, as the former Assistant Secretary of State for Far Eastern Affairs, Roger Hils-

man, has recommended, to maintain an "open
door" to the possibility of improved relations with
Communist China in the future. For a start we
must jar open our minds to certain realities about
China, of which the foremost is that there are not
really "two Chinas" but only one, mainland China,
and that it is ruled by Communists and likely to
remain so for the indefinite future. Once we accept
this fact, it becomes possible to reflect on the conditions under which it might be possible for us to
enter into relatively normal relations with mainland China. One condition, of course, must be
the abandonment by the Chinese Communists,
tacitly if not explicitly, of their intention to con-
quer and incorporate Taiwan. This seems unlikely
now, but far more surprising changes have occurred in politics, and it is quite possible that a new
generation of leaders in Peking and Taipei may put
a quiet end to the Chinese civil war, opening the
possibility of entirely new patterns of international
relations in the Far East.

Should such changes occur, they will open up
important opportunities for American policy, and
it is to be hoped that we will be able and willing
to take advantage of them. It seems possible, for
example, that an atmosphere of reduced tensions in
the Far East might make it possible to strengthen
world peace by drawing mainland China into
existing East-West agreements in such fields as

disarmament, trade, and educational exchange.

These are long-range prospects, which may or may not materialize. In the immediate future, we are confronted with possible changes in the Far East resulting from recent French diplomacy.

French recognition of Communist China, though untimely and carried out in a way that can hardly be considered friendly to the United States, may nonetheless serve a constructive long-term purpose by unfreezing a situation in which many countries, none more than the United States, are committed to inflexible policies by long-established commitments and the pressures of domestic public opinion. One way or another, the French initiative may help generate a new situation in which the United States, as well as other countries, will find it possible to re-evaluate its basic policies in the Far East.

The situation in Vietnam poses a far more pressing need for a re-evaluation of American policy. Other than withdrawal, which I do not think can be realistically considered under present circumstances, there are three options open to us in Vietnam: first, the continuation of the antiguerrilla war within South Vietnam, along with renewed American efforts to increase the military effectiveness of the South Vietnamese Army and the political effectiveness of the South Vietnamese Government; second, an attempt to end the war through negotiations for the neutralization of South Vietnam or of both North and South Vietnam; and finally, the expansion of the scale of the war, either by the direct commitment of American forces or by equipping the South Vietnamese armed forces to attack North Vietnamese territory, possibly by means of commando-type operations from the sea or air.

It is difficult to see how a negotiation, under present military circumstances, could lead to the termination of the war under conditions that would preserve the freedom of South Vietnam. It is extremely difficult for a party to a negotiation to achieve by diplomacy objectives which it has conspicuously failed to win by warfare. The hard fact of the matter is that our bargaining position is at present a weak one, and until the equation of advantages between the two sides has been substantially altered in our favor, there can be little prospect of a negotiated settlement which would secure the independence of a non-Communist South Vietnam.

Initiatives by France calling for the "neutralization" of Vietnam have tended to confuse the situation without altering it in any fundamental way. France could perhaps play a constructive mediating role if she were willing to consult and co-operate with the United States. For somewhat obscure reasons, however, France has chosen to take an independent initiative. This is puzzling to Americans, who recall that the United States contributed $2.5 billion to France's war in Indochina of a decade ago, which was one quarter to one third of the total cost of the conflict. Whatever its motivation, the problem posed by French intervention in Southeast Asia is that while France may set off an unforeseeable chain of events, she is neither a major military nor economic force in the Far East and is therefore unlikely to be able to control or greatly influence the events which her initiative may precipitate.

It seems clear that there are only two realistic options open to us in Vietnam in the immediate future: the expansion of the conflict in one way or another, or a renewed effort to bolster the capacity of the South Vietnamese to prosecute the war successfully on its present scale. The matter calls for continuing examination by responsible officials in the executive branch of our government. Until and unless they conclude that the military situation in South Vietnam, and the political situation in Southeast Asia, warrant the expansion of the war, or that the overall situation has changed sufficiently to establish some basis for a successful negotiation, it seems to me that we have no choice but to support the South Vietnamese Government and Army by the most effective means available. It should be clear to all concerned that the United

States will continue to defend its vital interests with respect to Vietnam.

Whatever strategic decisions are found necessary with respect to Vietnam—whether we decide to continue or intensify our present support for the South Vietnamese Government without expanding the scale of the operation, whether we seek a general negotiation without first trying to alter the military situation, or whether the war is carried to the territory of North Vietnam with a view to negotiating a reasonable settlement—I think we can be very clear now about what our objective is in Indochina and what it is not.

Our purpose is to uphold and strengthen the Geneva agreements of 1954 and 1962—that is to say, to establish viable, independent states in Indochina and elsewhere in Southeast Asia, which will be free of and secure from the domination of Communist China and Communist North Vietnam. I emphasize that we wish these nations to be *free of and secure from* domination by Peking and Hanoi, but not necessarily hostile to these regimes. Our objective is *not*—and in this I believe I am accurately expressing the official view of the United States Government as well as my own—to establish our own military power in Indochina or in any way to bring the nations of the Indochinese peninsula under our own domination or even to bring them into an American "sphere of influence."

(44)

. . .

These, I believe, are some, although by no means all, of the issues of foreign policy in which it is essential to re-evaluate long-standing ideas and commitments in the light of new and changing realities. In all the issues which I have discussed, and in others which will be discussed in subsequent chapters, American policy has to one degree or another been less effective than it might have been because of our national tendency to equate means with ends and therefore to attach a mythological sanctity to policies and practices which in themselves have no moral content or value except insofar as they contribute to the achievement of some valid national objective. I believe that we must try to overcome this excessive moralism, which binds us to old myths and blinds us to new realities and, worse still, leads us to regard new and unfamiliar ideas with fear and mistrust.

We must dare to think "unthinkable thoughts." We must learn to explore all of the options and possibilities that confront us in a complex and rapidly changing world. We must learn to welcome rather than fear the voices of dissent and not to recoil in horror whenever some heretic suggests that Castro may survive or that Khrushchev is not as bad a fellow as Stalin was. We must overcome our susceptibility to "shock"—a word which I wish could be banned from our newspapers and magazines and especially from the *Congressional Record*.

If Congress and public opinion are unduly susceptible to "shock," the executive branch, and particularly the Department of State, is subject to the malady of chronic and excessive caution. An effective foreign policy is one which concerns itself more with innovation abroad than with conciliation at home. A creative foreign policy—as President Truman, for one, knew—is not necessarily one which wins immediate general approval. It is sometimes necessary for leaders to do unpleasant and unpopular things, because, as Burke pointed out, the duty of the democratic politician to his constituents is not to comply with their every wish and preference, but to give them the benefit of, and to be held responsible for, the exercise of his own best judgment.

We must dare to think about "unthinkable things," because when things become "unthinkable," thinking stops and action becomes mindless. If we are to disabuse ourselves of old myths, and to act wisely and creatively upon the new realities of our time, we must think and talk about our problems with perfect freedom, remembering, as Woodrow Wilson said, that "The greatest freedom of speech is the greatest safety because, if a man is a fool, the best thing to do is to encourage him to advertise the fact by speaking."

II

The Foundations of
National Security

If our national security policies are to achieve their objective, which is to make the nation as secure as it can be in the nuclear age, they must be directed toward broader objectives than the expansion and refinement of a vast arsenal of weapons. A well-conceived national security program is one which concerns itself with the psychology as well as the technology of defense and deterrence. It must seek to bring some sanity and restraint into the relations of great nations which know, but do not always seem to feel and believe and act as though they know, that a decision made in anger or fear, or a simple mistake, could destroy at a stroke the effects of all the military preparations of a generation, and result in the incineration of tens of millions of people and the virtual destruction of human society.

National security does not and cannot depend on military power alone. Since the end of World War II American military power has been vastly increased by the development of nuclear weapons and ballistic missiles. At the same time, as Dr. Herbert York, the distinguished physicist and Director of Defense Research and Engineering under Presidents Eisenhower and Kennedy, has pointed out, our national security has been rapidly and inexorably diminishing. In the early 1950s the Soviet Union, had it been willing to pay the price of retaliation, could have inflicted some millions of casualties on the United States by an attack with bombers carrying atomic bombs. By the late 1950s the Soviets, at heavy retaliatory cost, could have attacked us with more and better bombers, inflicting some tens of millions of casualties. In the near future, if not at present, the Russians will be able to launch an attack on the United States using intercontinental missiles and bombers that would cause perhaps a hundred million casualties. The United States, of course, will be able to inflict at least equal, and probably much greater, losses in a retaliatory blow against the Soviet Union. As Dr.

York has said, "This steady decrease in national security was not the result of any inaction on our part, but simply the result of the systematic exploitation of the products of modern science and technology by the Soviet Union."[1]

There is no technical solution to the paradox of growing military power and decreasing national security. A nation's security depends upon its overall position in the world—on its political and economic strength as well as its military power, on its diplomacy and foreign trade, its alliances and associations, and on the character and quality of its internal life. Security depends in addition upon the general state of international relations, upon whether or not a nation has powerful enemies, and upon the character and policies of its enemies. Security, in short, is not merely a military and technological commodity, but a combination of many elements, all of which must be taken into account in the shaping of national policy.

The uncritical acceptance of a simple equation between security and armaments can only lead us into an accelerating arms race, mounting international tensions, and diminishing security. It is

[1] Statement by Dr. Herbert York, August 26, 1963, Hearings before the Committee on Foreign Relations, United States Senate, 88th Congress, First Session, *Nuclear Test Ban Treaty* (Washington, D. C.: U. S. Government Printing Office, 1963), pp. 761-762.

(49)

quite possible for us to possess overwhelming military superiority and still be confronted with the erosion of our power and influence in the world—if our alliance system is allowed to weaken, if confidence in our resolution is called into question, if our judgment is too often doubted, if our political and economic policies are ineffective, or if by ill-considered unilateral measures we provoke our adversaries into hostile countermeasures. We must therefore avoid giving undue weight to the political views of highly specialized technical experts whose experience and knowledge have only very limited relevance to the complexities of international relations. War, said Clemenceau, is too serious a business to be left to the generals. It is also too serious a business to be left to the nuclear physicists or, indeed, to anyone except an elected political leadership whose experience and competence is not in specific technical fields but in understanding the generality of the nation's problems, their effects upon each other, and the relative importance of one as against another.

None of this is intended to suggest that a high level of military power is anything less than essential as a deterrent to Communist aggression. It is intended to suggest, as Professor Marshall Shulman, a distinguished student of Soviet affairs, has put it, "that there may be a point beyond sufficiency at which purely military preoccupation may diminish rather than increase our security in the full sense of the word."[2]

History may teach us little about the present arms race, which, because it involves nuclear weapons, has possibilities for catastrophe unparalleled in the past. But one lesson is clear: a continuing arms race, accompanied by mounting fears and tensions, has frequently led to war in the past.

There is perhaps some instruction for us in the experience of Europe before 1914. None of the great powers of that era actually planned a major war, but each of the two major groupings, the Central Powers and the Entente Powers, was beset by fears of attack by the other. Fear grew into conviction as the two hostile alliances continued to arm against each other in a vain and desperate quest for security. Mutual fear generated the arms race, which in turn generated greater fear, until almost by accident Europe was plunged into general war.

Europe emerged broken and devastated from the war of 1914 and again from the Second World War, which was spawned by the consequences of the first. But the nations survived. The simple, compelling fact of our own time is that the world's great nations, and many of its smaller ones, almost certainly could not emerge as organized societies

[2] *Ibid.*, p. 798.

from a third World War, fought with nuclear weapons. It is this prospect, so obvious and yet so incomprehensible, that makes it essential for us to break out of the fatal cycle of fear and armaments and greater fear and finally war.

Measures such as the nuclear test ban treaty or the sale of American wheat to the Soviet Union or the conclusion of a new Soviet-American educational exchange agreement will not break the fatal cycle. Each is far too modest an effort to have more than a marginal effect on the conflict between the Communist and the free worlds. But taken together and faithfully observed, such steps can mitigate the fears and suspicions of the cold war, and perhaps in time may lead to further measures of limited accommodation. It is not likely—it is indeed all but inconceivable—that the conflict between communism and the free world can be resolved in our lifetimes. But the final resolution of the conflict, however vigorously we may desire and pursue it, is not an urgent matter. The world has always been beset by conflicts, religious and dynastic, national and ideological, and few have been resolved by means other than the evolution of history.

What is urgent for both the Communists and the free world is the prevention of nuclear war. This single objective, the survival of the civilized societies of the earth, is the one elemental interest which all nations have in common, and none more so than the United States and the Soviet Union, which, being the principal possessors of nuclear weapons, would also be their principal targets.

One of the great difficulties of devising and agreeing on rational measures to prevent nuclear war is what Raymond Aron has called "atomic incredulity," the fact that the consequences of such a war are almost beyond human comprehension. This "atomic incredulity" is apparent in our diplomacy and strategic thought, in our political discussions and our daily life. We speak with grave concern and feeling of a traffic fatality or a mine disaster or of the risks faced by an astronaut circling the earth, but we speak almost dispassionately of megaton weapons, of "big" bombs and "small" bombs, and of "showing the Russians that we're not afraid of war," as if these were rather ordinary subjects of discussion without any relationship to the destruction of our civilization and the death of hundreds of millions of people. Perhaps we would do well, in forming our "scientific" judgments of these weapons, to look again at the pictures of Hiroshima and Nagasaki, which were devastated by weapons of only fifteen or twenty kilotons. Perhaps we would do well, when we speak of "small" bombs of five or ten megatons, to remind ourselves that we are talking about weapons which, if used in warfare, would bring upon mankind a visitation of horror beyond anything ever approached or ever conceived in all of the wars of human history.

There is a kind of madness in the dialogue of the nuclear age, an incredulous response to terrors beyond our experience and imagination. There are few examples, in history, of nations acting rationally to prevent evils which they can foresee but have not actually experienced. Somehow, we must find a way, and encourage our adversaries to find a way, of bringing reason and conviction into our efforts to prevent nuclear war. Experience in this case is clearly not the best teacher, because few would survive to profit from the lesson.

The United States and Russia, with their vast territories and resources, do not need nuclear weapons to be the foremost nations of the world. Indeed, without nuclear weapons and ballistic missiles, Russia and the United States would be not only the strongest and richest nations of the world, as they are, but also the most secure and invulnerable to attack. By their acquisition of nuclear weapons the two great powers have destroyed the traditional advantages which size and resources had placed at their disposal. Their security now is a tenuous thing, depending solely on their power to deter attack and, ultimately, on sheer faith that each will respond with reason and restraint to the deterrent power of the other.

They are threatened further by the prospect of

proliferation. At some point in the future, Communist China and then many smaller nations may acquire nuclear weapons and the means of delivering them. The acquisition of nuclear weapons by small nations, if it occurs, will act as a great equalizer, giving them power out of all proportion to their size and resources, and further undermining the advantages of size and wealth enjoyed by great nations like the United States and the Soviet Union. The short-range effect of the acquisition of nuclear weapons by the two great powers was to increase their military stature. The long-range effect may be that the great powers, having undermined the traditional sources of power in which their advantage was overwhelming, will have to compete on terms approaching equality with nations that could never before have challenged them.[3]

For these reasons, the United States and the Soviet Union share an overriding *common* interest in the imposition of limitations and safeguards on nuclear weapons. Looked at in this way, such limited measures of arms control as the nuclear test ban treaty, by decelerating the arms race and reducing the pace of proliferation, can help the two great powers to recover some of the traditional advantages of great size and wealth. These advan-

---

[3] See Edmund O. Stillman and William Pfaff, *The New Politics* (New York: Coward McCann, 1961), pp. 138ff.

tages, so recklessly and unknowingly cast away by the scientific genius of the great powers themselves, can never be fully recovered. But it is clearly in our interests to attempt to mitigate the trend toward nuclear proliferation—a trend which, if realized, will place vast powers of destruction in the hands of small as well as great nations, of those who are reckless as well as those who are responsible, of those who have little to lose as well as those who have everything to lose.

There is no longer any validity in the Clausewitz doctrine of war as "a carrying out of policy with other means." Nuclear weapons have rendered it totally obsolete because the instrument of policy is now totally disproportionate to the end in view. Nuclear weapons have deprived force of its utility as an instrument of national policy, leaving the nuclear powers with vastly greater but far less useful power than they had before. So long as there is reason—not virtue, but simply reason—in the foreign policy of the great nations, nuclear weapons are not so much an instrument as an inhibition on policy.

By all available evidence, the Russians are no less aware of this than we. The memory of their 20 million dead in World War II is still fresh in the minds of most Russians. In a speech on July 19, 1963, Chairman Khrushchev castigated the Chinese Communists as "those who want to start a war against everybody. . . Do these men know," he asked, "that if all the nuclear warheads were touched off, the world would be in such a state that the survivors would envy the dead?" Or, commenting again in Hungary in April, 1964, on the equanimity with which the Chinese Communists spoke of nuclear war, Khrushchev expressed his opinion that "it is not from an excess of brains but from an absence of them that people say such things."

In the pursuit of its ambitions, whether by militant or peaceful means, the Soviet Union, like any other nation, is subject to the unending pressures for change imposed by time and circumstance. "Man," it has been said, "the supreme pragmatist, is a revisionist by nature."[4] Those who attribute to the Soviet leaders a permanent and unalterable determination to destroy the free societies of the West are crediting the Soviet Union with a strength and constancy of will that, so far as I know, has never been achieved by any nation.

There is, in fact, every reason to anticipate change, both within the Communist nations and in the relations between the Communist and the free nations. If there is any "law" of history, it is the inevitability and continuity of change. It is some-

[4] Eric Hansen, "Revisionism: Genesis and Prognosis" (unpublished paper).

times for the better, but often for the worse, and we cannot assume that the future evolution of the Communist world will be toward moderate and peaceful policies. But neither are we helpless and passive spectators to the course which the Communist nations follow. We have the means and resources to influence events in the Soviet Union and in other bloc countries. Our ability to put those means to effective use depends in no small measure on our willingness to go beyond a rigidly ideological view of communism and to deal with the Communist countries as the national entities which they are, each with special national interests and aspirations.

If we look at the Communist bloc objectively, and not through the distorting prism of ideological hostility, we can see that important and encouraging changes have already taken place. We perceive that Soviet society and the Soviet economy are becoming highly complex, too complex to be completely and efficiently controlled by a highly centralized dictatorship. We perceive that under the pressures of growing complexity a degree of economic decentralization has taken place, that the police terror of the Stalin era has been abated, that the Central Committee of the Communist Party may even be developing under Khrushchev into a kind of rudimentary parliamentary body. And most important of all, as I pointed out in

(58)

Chapter I, the unity of the Communist bloc has been disrupted, and we find ourselves confronted with a growing diversity of national outlooks and policies, ranging from the harsh orthodoxy of Communist China to the pragmatism of the Soviet Union, the nationalism of Poland and Hungary, and the astonishing diplomatic independence of Rumania.

There are those who maintain that the only valid test of altered Soviet policies must be the explicit repudiation of those tenets of Marxist ideology that call for world revolution and the universal victory of communism. To ask for overt renunciation of a cherished doctrine is to expect too much of human nature. Men do not repudiate the doctrines and dogmas to which they have sworn their loyalty. Instead they rationalize, revise, and reinterpret them to meet new needs and new circumstances, all the while protesting that their heresy is the purest orthodoxy.

Something of this nature is now occurring in the Soviet Union. Khrushchev has not repudiated Marx and Lenin; on the contrary, he vows his fealty to their doctrines at every opportunity. But his "orthodoxy" has not deterred him from some striking interpretations of the scriptures. Contrast, for example, the Marxist-Leninist emphasis on discipline and self-sacrifice and revolution with Khrushchev's famous words in Budapest in April, 1964:

"The important thing is that we should have more to eat—good goulash—schools, housing, and ballet. How much more do these things give to the enlargement of man's life? It is worth fighting and working for these things." Or contrast the Marxist-Leninist principle of relentless struggle for the universal victory of communism with Khrushchev's answer to his own rhetorical question as to whether the Soviet Union should help the French working class to take over power. "Who asked us to mix in their affairs?" was his reply. "What do we know about them?"

The attribution of an unalterable will and constancy to Soviet policy has been a serious handicap to our own policy. It has restricted our ability to gain insights into the realities of Soviet society and Soviet foreign policy. It has denied us valuable opportunities to take advantage of changing conditions in the Communist world and to encourage changes which would reduce the Communist threat to the free world. We have overestimated the ability of the Soviets to pursue malevolent aims, without regard to time or circumstances, and, in so doing, we have underestimated our own ability to influence Soviet behavior.

A stigma of heresy has been attached to suggestions by American policy-makers that Soviet policy can change or that it is sometimes altered in response to our own. But it is a fact that in the

wake of the failure of the aggressive policies of the
Stalin period, the Soviet leaders have gradually
shifted to a policy of peaceful, or competitive, coexistence with the West. This policy confronts us
with certain dangers but also with important opportunities if we are wise enough to take advantage of them.

The abrupt change in the Soviet position which
made possible the signing of the nuclear test ban
treaty in 1963 appears to have been motivated by
the general failure of competitive coexistence as
practiced in the last few years and by a number
of specific problems, both foreign and domestic.
The most conspicuous of these is the public erup-
tion of the dispute with Communist China. In addition, the Soviet leaders have been troubled by
economic difficulties at home, particularly in agri-
culture, by the increasingly insistent demands of
the Russian people for more and better food,
clothing, and housing, and by difficulties between
the regime and Soviet intellectuals and artists; by
increasing centrifugal tendencies in Eastern Europe, aggravated by the dismaying contrast with
an increasingly prosperous and powerful Western
Europe; and by the negligible rewards of Soviet
diplomacy and economic aid in Asia and Africa.

The most crucial failure of Soviet policy has
been in its dealings with the West. Contrary to
Soviet expectations of a few years ago, it has

proven impossible to extract concessions from the West on Berlin and Central Europe by nuclear diplomacy. Thwarted in Europe, Khrushchev embarked in the fall of 1962 on the extremely dangerous adventure of placing missiles in Cuba, hoping, it would seem, to force a solution in Berlin and an unfreezing of Central Europe. The debacle in Cuba led the Soviet leaders to a major reappraisal of their policies.

That reappraisal has apparently resulted in a decision to seek a relaxation of tensions with the West. The nuclear test ban treaty and subsequent limited agreements with the West were clearly calculated to serve that purpose. In addition, the tone of Soviet diplomacy has changed; in matters ranging from Cuba to Vietnam, vituperation has been muted and the Russians have passed up a number of opportunities to quarrel with the United States.

From the Soviet point of view, a limited *détente* with the West appears to offer certain clear advantages. Three reasons for seeking improved relations with the West seem of major importance. First and foremost is the genuine fear of nuclear war which the Soviets share with the West, all the more since the United States demonstrated in the Cuban crisis that it was prepared to use nuclear weapons to defend its vital interests. Secondly, in the mounting conflict with the Chinese, the Soviet Union can claim a success for its policies of "peaceful coexistence" and, more important, can use the world-wide popularity of the test ban and other arms-control measures to strengthen its position both in the Communist bloc and in the non-Communist underdeveloped countries, thereby further isolating the Chinese. Thirdly, Khrushchev appears to be interested in measures which will permit a leveling off, and perhaps a reduction, of weapons expenditures in order to be able to divert scarce resources for meeting some of the demands of the Russian people for a better life.

In an article written shortly after the signing of the test ban treaty, Professor Zbigniew Brzezinski, Director of Columbia University's Research Institute on Communist Affairs, interpreted the Soviet adherence to the test ban treaty as follows: "Khrushchev's acceptance of an 'atmosphere-only' test ban strongly suggests a major Soviet reassessment of the world situation and an implicit acknowledgment that Soviet policies of the last few years have failed. The Soviet leaders have evidently concluded that the general world situation is again in a 'quiescent' stage. Instead of dissipating Soviet resources in useless revolutionary efforts, or missile adventures of the Cuban variety, they will probably concentrate on consolidating their present position."[5]

. . .

[5] Zbigniew Brzezinski, "After the Test Ban," *The New Republic,* August 31, 1963, p. 18.

If the relaxation of tensions is conceived by the Soviets as an interlude in which to consolidate their position, strengthen their power base, and then renew their aggressive policies against the West, is it wise for us to grant them this interlude? It is indeed wise, for two main reasons: first, because it will provide the West with an identical opportunity to strengthen the power base of the free world; and secondly, because it will generate conditions in which the Soviet and Communist bloc peoples will be emboldened to step up their demands for peace and a better life, conditions which the Soviet leadership will find it exceedingly difficult to alter.

From the point of view of the West, an interlude of relaxed world tensions will provide a splendid opportunity to strengthen the foundations of the security of the free world—if only we will use it. First of all, we can use the opportunity to bring greater unity and prosperity to the Atlantic community—by seeking means of resolving our differences over the control of nuclear weapons and by negotiating extensive tariff reductions under the terms of the American Trade Expansion Act of 1962. Secondly, we can re-invigorate our efforts to strengthen the free nations of Asia, Africa, and Latin America by providing a more discriminating and intelligent program of economic assistance and by encouraging co-operative free-world aid programs through such agencies as the International Development Association. Finally, we can use a period of relaxed tensions to focus energy and resources on our long-neglected needs here at home—on the expansion and improvement of our public education, on generating greater economic growth and full employment, on the conservation of our resources and the renewal of our cities.

All of these lines of action have a direct and vital bearing on our national security. If we pursue them with vigor and determination, I think it can be confidently predicted that the free world will be the major beneficiary of a period of relaxed world tension, with a power base so strengthened that the margin of free-world superiority over the Communist bloc will be substantially widened.

The other great advantage to the West of a period of relaxed tensions is that it may release long-suppressed pressures for peace and the satisfaction of civilian needs within the Soviet bloc. Public opinion, even in a dictatorship like the Soviet Union, is an enormously powerful force which no government can safely defy for too long or in too many ways. Russian public opinion is overwhelmingly opposed to war and overwhelmingly in favor of higher wages, of better food, clothing, and housing, and of all the good things of life in a modern industrial society. The Russian *people* may well turn out to be a powerful ally of the free nations, who also want peace and prosperity. It is quite possible that a thaw in Soviet-American relations, even though conceived by the Soviet leadership as a temporary pause, could lead gradually to an entirely new relationship. Motives have a way of becoming lost as the actions to which they give rise generate new attitudes and new and unforeseen motives. Pressed by the demands of an increasingly assertive public opinion, the Soviet leaders may find new reasons to continue a policy of peace and accommodation with the West. Step by step their revolutionary zeal may diminish, as they find that a peaceful and affluent national existence is not really so tragic a fate as they had imagined.

No one knows whether Soviet society will actually evolve along these lines, but the trend of Soviet history suggests that it is by no means impossible. "Indeed, the most striking characteristic of recent Soviet foreign policy," Professor Shulman has pointed out, "has been the way in which policies undertaken for short-term, expediential purposes have tended to elongate in time, and become embedded in doctrine and political strategy."[6]

[6] Statement by Professor Marshall Shulman, August 26, 1963, Hearings before the Committee on Foreign Relations, United States Senate, 88th Congress, First Session, *Nuclear Test Ban Treaty* (Washington, D.C.: U.S. Government Printing Office, 1963), p. 797.

It is possible, I believe, for the West to encourage a hopeful direction in Soviet policy. We can seek to strengthen Russian public opinion as a brake against dangerous policies by conveying accurate information about Western life and Western aims, and about the heavy price that both sides are paying for the cold war. We can make it clear to the Russians that they have nothing to fear from the West so long as they respect the rights and independence of other nations. We can suggest to them at every possible opportunity, both by persuasion and by example, that there is no greater human vanity than the assumption that one's own values have universal validity, and no enterprise more certain of failure than the attempt to impose the preferences of a single society on an unwilling world. And finally, we can encourage them to recognize, as we must never fail to recognize ourselves, that adventures born of passion are soon severed from their lofty aims, turning idealism into barbarism and men into demons.

On November 14, 1860, Alexander Hamilton Stephens, who subsequently became Vice-President of the Southern Confederacy, delivered an address to the Georgia Legislature which bears wisdom for our own time. Appealing to his colleagues to delay the withdrawal of Georgia from the Union, Stephens said of the prospective secession: "It may be that out of it we may become greater and more prosperous, but I am candid and sincere in telling you that I fear if we yield to passion, and without sufficient cause shall take that step, that instead of becoming greater or more peaceful, prosperous, and happy—instead of becoming Gods, we will become demons, and at no distant day commence cutting one another's throats. This is my apprehension. Let us, therefore, whatever we do, meet these difficulties, great as they are, like wise and sensible men, and consider them in the light of all the consequences which may attend our action."[7]

The purpose of a realistic foreign policy is not to end the cold war but to modify it, not to resolve the conflict between communism and freedom—a goal which is almost certainly beyond the reach of the present generation—but to remove some of the terror and passion from it. The progress thus far achieved and now in prospect has been small in substance, in the sense that it has brought us scarcely closer to a solution of such great problems as the arms race and the division of Germany. But in another sense—the extremely important psychological sense—it may be that we are doing better than we know. The ultimate criterion of the importance of any issue is its im-

[7] Alexander Hamilton Stephens, "Secession," in *Modern Eloquence* (New York: P. F. Collier & Sons, 1928), Vol. II, p. 203.

plications for war and peace. The division of Germany is a most important issue in itself, but its global and historical significance, like that of the arms race, is that it has a critical bearing on whether we shall have war or peace. If, by a series of agreements on issues which in substance are much less important than the division of Germany and the arms race—such agreements as the test ban treaty, reductions in the output of fissionable materials, or the opening of consulates and airline connections—we succeed in creating a *state of mind* in which neither side considers war as a likely eventuality or as a real option for itself except under radically changed conditions, then in fact we will have progressed toward precisely the same objective which a German settlement or a general disarmament agreement would help to achieve—a world substantially free of the threat of nuclear incineration.

The point which I am trying, imperfectly, to make is that in our quest for world peace the *alteration of attitudes* is no less important, perhaps more important, than the resolution of issues. It is in the minds of men, after all, that wars are spawned; to act upon the human mind, regardless of the issue or occasion for doing so, is to act upon the source of conflict and the potential source of redemption and reconciliation. It would seem, therefore, that there may be important new things to be learned about international relations through the scholarship of psychologists and pyschiatrists.

When all is said and done, when the abstractions and subtleties of political science have been exhausted, there remain the most basic unanswered questions about war and peace and why we contest the issues we contest and why we even care about them. As Aldous Huxley has written: "There may be arguments about the best way of raising wheat in a cold climate or of re-afforesting a denuded mountain. But such arguments never lead to organized slaughter. Organized slaughter is the result of arguments about such questions as the following: Which is the best nation? The best religion? The best political theory? The best form of government? Why are other people so stupid and wicked? Why can't they see how good and intelligent we are? Why do they resist our beneficent efforts to bring them under our control and make them like ourselves?"[8]

In our search for answers to the complex questions of war and peace, we come ultimately to the paradox of man himself, which I have never heard better expressed than in a one-page essay called "Man," written by an American hill-country philosopher whose writings suggest strongly the style and thought of Mark Twain. It reads as follows:

[8] Aldous Huxley, "The Politics of Ecology" (pamphlet, published by The Center for the Study of Democratic Institutions, Santa Barbara, California, 1963), p. 6.

Man is a queer animal, like the beasts of the fields, the fowls of the air, and the fishes of the sea, he came into this world without his consent and is going out the same way.

At birth he is one of the most helpless creatures in all existence. He can neither walk, talk, swim nor crawl, and has but two legs while most other animals have four legs. Unlike other animals he has no covering for his body to protect it against the bite or sting of poisonous insects, tooth or claw of ferocious beasts save a little hair which appears about his body only in patches.

With all his limitations he yet has one advantage over animals—the power of reason, but history shows that he often discards that for superstition. Of all the animals on earth, man has shown himself to be the most cruel and brutal. He is the only animal that will create instruments of death for his own destruction.

Man is the only animal on all the earth that has ever been known to burn its young as a sacrifice to appease the wrath of some imaginary deity. He is the only one that will build homes, towns and cities at such a cost in sacrifice and suffering and turn around and destroy them in war.

He is the only animal that will gather his

fellows together in creeds, clans, and nations, line them up in companies, regiments, armies, and get glory out of their slaughter. Just because some king or politician told him to.

Man is the only creature in all existence that is not satisfied with the punishment he can inflict on his fellows while here, but had to invent a hell of fire and brimestone in which to burn them after they are dead.

Where he came from, or when, or how, or where he is going after death he does not know, but he hopes to live again in ease and idleness where he can worship his gods and enjoy himself, watching his fellow creatures wriggle and writhe in eternal flames down in hell.

The root question, for which I must confess I have no answer, is how and why it is that so much of the energy and intelligence that men could use to make life better for themselves is used instead to make life difficult and painful for other men. When the subtleties of strategy and power and diplomatic method have all been explained, we are still left with the seemingly unanswerable question of how and why it is that we *care* about such things, which are so remote from the personal satisfactions that bring pleasure and grace and fulfillment into our lives.

The paradoxes of human nature are eternal and perhaps unanswerable, but I do think we know enough about elemental human needs to be able to apply certain psychological principles in our efforts to alleviate the tensions of the cold war.

In this connection, I would suggest that a great deal—more than one would suspect—depends upon the *manner* in which we seek to negotiate reasonable agreements with the Russians. We must remember that we are not dealing with automatons whose sole function in life is to embody an ideology and a party line, but with human beings—people who, like ourselves, have special areas of pride, prejudice, and sensitivity. I have found, for example, as have others who have discussed current issues with Soviet officials and citizens, that the whole trend of a conversation can be influenced by the way in which you begin it. If you confront them at the outset with an attack on the harshness of their ideology, the shortcomings of their economy, or the excesses of their dictatorship, you are likely to be rewarded with an outburst of chauvinism and vituperation about American policy and practices. There are those who find such encounters emotionally satisfying, but no one can deny that they are singularly barren of productive results.

If, on the other hand, you start out with a compliment about the successes of Soviet society—

and there have been a few—or with a candid reference to the shortcomings of our own society—and there have also been a few of these—then it often happens that the response is surprisingly expansive and conciliatory. You are likely to hear an admission that everything, after all, is not perfect in the Soviet Union, and that there are even a few things about America that are admirable and worthy of imitation.

The compliments in themselves are of little importance. But the candor and the cordiality are of great importance. As any good businessman knows, they set a tone and an atmosphere in which emotion gives way to reason and it becomes possible to do business, to move on from cordial generalities to specific negotiations. They generate that minimum of mutual confidence which is absolutely essential for reaching concrete agreements. Under existing circumstances, no one can expect such agreements to be more than modest accommodations which are clearly in the mutual interest; but they are at least a start toward more significant arrangements, and as I have already suggested, the critical question of war and peace may have less to do with the specifications of agreements than with the attitudes they engender and the attitudes they dispel.

"Frightened, hostile individuals tend to behave in ways which aggravate their difficulties instead of resolving them," says the distinguished psychiatrist Dr. Jerome D. Frank, "and frightened, hostile nations seem to behave similarly."[9] A nation, like an individual, Dr. Frank suggests, is likely to respond to a feared rival by breaking off communications, by provocative behavior, or by taking measures which promise immediate relief, regardless of their ultimate consequences.

Among the psychiatrically constructive techniques which might be used to cope with the destructive emotions of the cold war, Dr. Frank suggests the following: that we give Russian views our respectful attention as one way of making the Russians more receptive to ours; that we enormously increase communications between the Communist and the free worlds through cultural, scientific, agricultural, and student exchange programs; that we engage in co-operative activities that will enable both sides to achieve desired goals neither can as readily achieve alone—such activities as joint projects in space exploration or in building health services throughout the world, or such enterprises as the possible Central American canal consortium referred to in Chapter I.

Through such means we may strive to break through the ideological passions and national animosities that fill men's minds with destructive zeal and blind them to what Aldous Huxley called the

[9] Letter from Dr. Frank to the author, September 13, 1960.

simple human preference for life and peace. Through such means we may strive to build strong foundations for our national security and, indeed, for the security of all peoples.

We must bring to bear all the resources of human knowledge and invention to build viable foundations of security in the nuclear age—the resources of political science and history, of economics and sociology, of psychology and literature and the arts. It is not enough to seek security through armaments or even through ingenious schemes of disarmament; nor is it enough to seek security through schemes for the transfer of territories or for the deployment and redeployment of forces. Security is a state of mind rather than a set of devices and arrangements. The latter are important because they contribute, but only to the extent that they contribute, to generating a *psychological process* in which peoples and statesmen come increasingly to think of war as undesirable and unfeasible.

It is this *process* that has critical importance for our security. Whether we advance it by seeking a settlement on Berlin or a new disarmament agreement, by the opening of consulates or by a joint enterprise in space, is less important than that the process be advanced. Our emphasis at any one time should be on those issues which seem most likely to be tractable and soluble. As long as we are by one means or another cultivating a world-wide state of mind in which peace is favored over war, we are doing the most effective possible thing to strengthen the foundations of our security. And only when such a state of mind is widely prevalent in the world will the kind of unprecedented political creativity on a global scale which has been made necessary by the invention of nuclear weapons become possible as well.

The cold war and all the other national rivalries of our time are not likely to evaporate in our lifetimes. The major question of our time is not how to end these conflicts but whether we can find some way to conduct them without resorting to weapons that will resolve them once and for all by wiping out the contestants. A generation ago we were speaking of "making the world safe for democracy." Having failed of this in two World Wars, we must now seek ways of making the world reasonably safe for the continuing contest between those who favor democracy and those who oppose it. It is a modest aspiration, but it is a sane and realistic one for a generation which, having failed of grander things, must now look to its own survival.

Extreme nationalism and dogmatic ideology are luxuries that the human race can no longer afford. It must turn its energies now to the politics of survival. If we do so, we may find in time that we can do better than just survive. We may find that the simple human preference for life and peace has an inspirational force of its own, less intoxicating perhaps than the sacred abstractions of nation and ideology, but far more relevant to the requirements of human life and human happiness.

There are, to be sure, risks in such an approach. There is an element of trust in it, and we can be betrayed. But human life is fraught with risks, and the behavior of the sane man is not the avoidance of all possible danger but the weighing of greater against lesser risks and of risks against opportunities.

We have an opportunity at present to try to build stronger foundations for our national security than armaments alone can ever provide. That opportunity lies in a policy of encouraging the development of a habit of peaceful and civilized contacts between ourselves and the Communist bloc. I believe that this opportunity must be pursued, with reason and restraint, with due regard for the pitfalls involved and for the possibility that our efforts may fail, but with no less regard for the promise of a safer and more civilized world. In the course of this pursuit, both we and our adversaries may find it possible one day to break through the barriers of nationalism and ideology and to approach each other in something of the spirit of Pope John's words to Khrushchev's son-in-law: "They tell me you are an atheist. But you will not refuse an old man's blessing for your children."

III

Atlantic Partnership and the Gaullist Challenge

Until January, 1963, when General de Gaulle fore-closed the admission of Great Britain to the European Common Market, the North Atlantic nations were proceeding apace in the development of a working concert of free nations. In an atmosphere of hope and creativity the Western democracies took a series of practical measures, beginning with the Marshall Plan and the NATO Treaty, and culminating in the establishment of the European Economic Community, which seemed likely to exorcise the West's ancient malady of nationalism and to lead the West to a greater degree of unity than it has known at any time in the modern era. This remarkable trend has now been arrested, perhaps permanently, perhaps only momentarily, as a result of the policy of France under President de Gaulle.

Since January 14, 1963, when President de Gaulle pronounced Great Britain unsuited for membership in the European Economic Community, the Atlantic democracies have been engaged in a debate of historic importance on the future organization of Europe and the West. The issue is between a Gaullist concept of a European confederation of sovereign states linked to Great Britain, America, and other Western nations by general assurances of friendship and support, and an Atlantic concept of a European federation with limited supranational powers bound to the United States and other Atlantic countries by specifically defined mutual obligations in the fields of defense, trade, and political organization. For reasons which I shall attempt to make clear, I believe that the Atlantic concept contains by far the greater hope and opportunity for the free nations of the West.

In the eighteenth century the Western world was conscious of its common civilization. America was linked to England politically and to Europe as well as England by powerful bonds of commerce and of culture. There were accepted rules and principles of international behavior, and even the frequent dynastic and colonial wars that were fought were limited conflicts for limited purposes that did not seek to overturn the existing order of nations and societies.

There followed, in the wake of the American and French revolutions and the Napoleonic wars, an age of nationalism which brought with it an emphasis on the self-centered nation and its autonomous growth. In America, nationalism took the form of self-imposed isolation from the rest of the world while we concentrated on developing the resources of the rich North American continent. In Europe, nineteenth-century nationalism was at first a unifying force and one which was closely associated with democratic and humanitarian ideas; but in the last decades of the century there developed a growing divergence between democracy and nationalism as the latter became strident, aggressive, and militarist. The bonds of common civilization were increasingly strained by the rise of militant nationalism. In the twentieth century these bonds were shattered and Western civilization all but destroyed itself in the ferocity of two World Wars. Only the United States, drawn reluctantly from its isolation into the vortex of conflict, emerged from these great trials strong and intact.

The convulsions of the World Wars had three

immediate consequences: first, Western Europe emerged physically and spiritually exhausted, its economy shattered and its peoples demoralized; secondly, Russia emerged as a virile and ambitious power, posing a vast new danger for the West with a world policy of aggressive totalitarianism; thirdly, the nationalism which had all but consumed the West spread through Asia, Africa, and Latin America, resulting in the rapid disintegration of the old Western empires.

During the immediate postwar years the United States, as the only remaining center of strength in the Western world, bore the full burden of defending the West against the new Communist imperialism. With our monopoly of atomic weapons and our vast economic power, we were able to stem the tide of Communist expansion and to provide the material resources for beginning the reconstruction of the Western community. American leadership, through the Marshall Plan and the formulation of the NATO Alliance, carried Europe through the immediate crisis of the postwar years and enabled the European nations to begin to rebuild their shattered economies.

Through its aid and support for Western Europe, the United States moved to rejoin the Atlantic community from which it had separated in the eighteenth century, while a new generation of Europeans began to reconstruct the bonds of community that had been severed by a generation of tyranny and war. A slow and painful trend toward unification thereupon took hold, going beyond reconciliation toward the possible realization of the ancient and elusive dream of a genuine federation of Europe.

While a few tentative efforts have been made toward the establishment of formal political institutions, the main thrust of the drive toward European unity has been through practical measures of co-operation in specific functional areas. In 1947 and 1948 the necessity for co-ordinated efforts to achieve economic recovery led to the formation of the Organization for European Economic Cooperation to superivse and co-ordinate the uses of American aid under the Marshall Plan. The Communist seizure of power in Czechoslovakia in 1948 was followed by the formation of NATO in 1949, the grand alliance of the Western nations. In 1952 the European Coal and Steel Community was launched, placing the coal and steel production of France, West Germany, Italy, and Benelux under a supranational High Authority. In 1957 the Six continental countries signed the Treaty of Rome creating the European Economic Community, or Common Market. In 1957 they also formed EURATOM for co-operation in the development of atomic energy.

The United States and Canada joined with the

European countries in the Organization for Economic Cooperation and Development, established in 1961 for the purpose of enabling the Atlantic countries (and now Japan as well) to concert their monetary policies and to co-ordinate their domestic economic programs. A Development Assistance Committee under the OECD is intended to co-ordinate free-world aid programs to the underdeveloped countries, and to encourage an equitable distribution of responsibilities in this field among the advanced industrial nations of the free world. In addition to joining these international institutions, the United States enacted the Trade Expansion Act of 1962, with the expectation that its liberal provisions for tariff reduction would lead to a great expansion in trade between Europe and America, and thereafter to a general expansion of world trade and economic growth.

The "grand design" for Atlantic partnership envisioned the concurrent development of two sets of relationships: an evolving federation of Europe with institutions vested with specified supranational powers and a broader set of arrangements for linking Europe and America to each other in a close military, political, and economic partnership. Underlying this concept of a double pattern of relationships were three basic expectations: first, that the "Europe of the Six" would not wish to remain exclusive but would welcome the membership of Great Britain and other Western European countries; secondly, that a united Europe, whatever its composition, would not develop an exclusive nationalism of its own, but would welcome new arrangements with the United States and Canada for the common defense, the expansion of trade, and close co-operation in the field of aid to the underdeveloped countries; and thirdly, that the United States would enter into such co-operative arrangements even though they involved limited but real incursions on American sovereignty, particularly in the area of sharing responsibility for the control of nuclear weapons and delivery systems.

These expectations, it is now clear, were not well founded, nor are they likely to be fulfilled in the near future. General de Gaulle's policies have shown us that our hopes for an Atlantic partnership were premature and overly optimistic.

It does not follow, however, that these hopes cannot be retrieved and eventually realized. It remains to be seen whether General de Gaulle has actually reversed the tendency of postwar history or merely arrested it. "History" is not a divine force; it is the instrument of those who make it. I believe that it is within our power to influence events, and I think it regrettable that many knowledgable Americans are accepting the prospect of a general revival of European nationalism, not as something which they regard as desirable, but rather as something which they deem to be historically "inevitable." Perhaps it is, but until it is clearly seen to be so, until we are quite sure that our own ability to influence events is insufficient, it seems to me that we would do well to continue our efforts on behalf of a program which is far more creative and far more promising for the future of Western civilization than a reversion to the nationalism of the past.

The challenge of Atlantic partnership is a challenge to the most persistent and destructive myth of the last two centuries of Western history: the myth that the modern nation-state is a spiritual organism with a sanctity that transcends the individual. In reality, the modern nation is the product of the historical evolution of human groups from their tribal beginnings to ever larger forms of social organization, not as the result of some mystical force of history, but in response to very *practicable* economic, military, and political needs. Until the twentieth century the building of nations represented a broadening of human bonds, but in the modern world of peoples made interdependent by scientific and technological revolution, the mythology of the absolutely sovereign and self-sufficient nation delimits the bonds among men, confining them within political communities no longer capable of satisfying the requirements of security and economic growth. Indeed, the concept of national sovereignty has become in our time a principle of international anarchy. If the real needs of the West and of the world are to be met, neither sovereignty nor national self-determination can be absolute. Our survival in this century may well turn out to depend upon whether we succeed in transferring at least some small part of our feelings of loyalty and responsibility from the sovereign nation to some larger political community.

The concept of Atlantic partnership is rooted in these realities. It may indeed exceed our capacity to extend the frontiers of our loyalty, and if realized it may still fall short of the needs of the nuclear age. But the Atlantic idea represents a reasonable accommodation between an intolerable nationalism and an unattainable world community, between the deeply ingrained habits that bind us to the nation-state and the unprecedented dangers that must drive us eventually to seek our safety in a community of mankind.

In his address of July 4, 1962, at Philadelphia, President Kennedy stated the case on which the Atlantic idea must stand or fall: "Acting on our own," he said, "by ourselves, we cannot establish justice throughout the world; we cannot ensure its domestic tranquility, or provide for its common defense, or promote its general welfare, or secure the blessings of liberty to ourselves and our posterity. But joined with other free nations, we can do all this and more. We can assist the developing nations to throw off the yoke of poverty. We can balance our world-wide trade and payments at the highest possible level of growth. We can mount a deterrent powerful enough to deter any aggression. . . ."

Although it is clear that the objectives of current French policy are different from those defined by President Kennedy at Philadelphia, it is far from clear what President de Gaulle's objectives are. It is exceedingly difficult to perceive the shape and character of a "Gaullist" Europe from the General's public pronouncements. We have been told that the postwar era is at an end and that the Gaullist design is built on that reality; that the Atlantic partnership idea is only a disguise for American "hegemony" in Europe; that this "hegemony," which is equated with Soviet domination of Eastern Europe, is intolerable and must soon end; that France and Europe (the terms seems to be used interchangeably) have a destiny and "personality" of their own which must not be diluted by "Anglo-Saxon" admixtures; and that Europe must aspire to be "Europe from the Atlantic to the Urals."

This, I believe, is an only slightly editorialized rendering of the Gaullist program as it has thus far been enunicated. In its present state of definition it seems more a mystique than a program. It may be that President de Gaulle, in his own good time, will give content to his vision of Europe and of the world. It may be that he will go beyond elegant disquisitions on the pride and personality of nations and proceed to suggest the kind of institutions which might bind together a confederation of sovereign European states, and the kind of political and economic relations which may bind or divide Europe from the overseas democracies.

Until the French objectives are clarified, it seems to me impossible to form definitive opinions about the Gaullist program. I am at a loss to understand the enthusiasm which current French policies seem to have inspired in some of our most respected students of international affairs, some of whom have gone so far as to adopt as their own the rather special Gaullist vocabulary, in which Russia and the United States are referred to as "hegemonies" rather than nations, and it is considered a most striking insight to observe that the postwar era is at an end or that France, in some mystic way, must be France. I am bound to recognize that there are things which may have escaped my attention or understanding, but with this important qualification: it does seem to me that General de

Gaulle's concept of the future of Europe has not been defined beyond stirring generalizations, and that until it is we have to reserve judgment on its desirability, feasibility, and inevitability.

Whatever their design for the future may be, General de Gaulle's operating policies suggest a view of world politics which is profoundly reactionary in the historical sense, tending back toward the nationalism which for so long divided the West against itself and which spawned the two World Wars. They are also recognizable as one of those periodic outbursts of brilliant and creative energy which have occurred from time to time in the history of the French nation. I suspect that much of the widespread admiration for General de Gaulle's policies has been inspired by his own personality and by the skill with which his policies are executed, rather than by their inherent wisdom.

In a series of press conferences and other public statements beginning with his well-remembered press conference of January 14, 1963, President de Gaulle has made a number of general statements which France's friends and allies can heartily endorse. In his press conference of July 29, 1963, for example, he declared that "the fundamental factors of French-American relations are friendship and alliance"; that this friendship is "an outstanding psychological reality in keeping with the nature of the two countries"; "that the Atlantic Alliance is an 'elemental necessity,'" and that within it France and the United States have a "capital responsibility."

These broad principles are as valid in content as they are eloquent in expression. President de Gaulle is also correct in warning us against "depicting each scratch as an incurable wound." At the same time, I think it appropriate for us to remind France, and the other countries of Western Europe, that a viable alliance depends on common policies as well as common objectives, on co-operation in fact as well as agreement in principle. If the Western Alliance is to be a meaningful factor in world politics, it must be built on more than bonds of friendship and high regard. It requires working agreements for political consultation and the command and disposition of military forces, for economic co-operation and the lowering of trade barriers.

It is on this level of practical co-operation that French policy has been deeply disappointing to France's allies. It is a policy which, if long continued, could lead to the disruption of the Western Alliance, if not by open repudiation, then by abnegation in detail.

A distinguished young professor of politics once told me that I was making what he called a "useful and necessary" effort to understand what was going on in the Soviet Union, and he urged me to make a similar effort with regard to France. I believe this suggesstion was entirely appropriate. It is certainly important for Americans to make an effort to understand the political, military, and historical motivations of current French policy. It is no less important for France to make a commensurate effort with regard to the problems and objectives of American policy.

A meaningful dialogue between France and the United States must begin with an examination of the profound impact on both countries of the events of the last twenty-five years.

France, as President de Gaulle has pointed out, was "materially and morally destroyed by the collapse of 1940" and by the discreditable Vichy interlude.[1] Following the liberation, France was beset by political and economic weaknesses at home and by the long and fruitless struggles in Indo-China and Algeria. All this time France was forced into a relationship of military and economic dependence on the United States, a deeply humiliating experience for a great and proud nation. Since General de Gaulle's return to power in 1958, France, with astonishing speed, has recovered her political stability, ended the colonial wars, and returned to vibrant economic health.

As a result of this great resurgence, France has

[1] Press Conference, July 29, 1963.

ended her economic dependency on the United States, and reasserted herself with vigor and confidence as one of the great nations of Europe. These developments are as welcome to the United States as they are to France, but the memory of defeat and dependency remains, and one perceives in current French policy an excess of pride and assertiveness that is entirely natural for a great nation which was struck down and has only recently recovered its dignity and strength. It is natural for France to be acutely sensitive and proud at this juncture in her history, and it is even natural for her to feel resentment toward those who liberated her and then sustained her through the years of weakness.

It is natural but it does not represent an accurate interpretation of the events of the last twenty years. The United States did not *wish* to become the protector and benefactor of Europe after World War II. Still less did it wish to dominate Europe. Through the Marshall Plan and subsequent programs of military and economic support, America came to Europe's assistance for the simple but compelling reason that Europe was momentarily incapable of sustaining itself, and its recovery was vital to the interests of the United States. America's postwar policy toward Europe was by no means an exercise in pure altruism but neither was it an effort to dominate Europe. It was a policy of enlightened mutual interest, and its success has brought signal benefits to both Europe and America.

The issues on which France and the United States now disagree are the outgrowth of the *success* of our postwar policies. They have grown out of Europe's brilliant recovery from World War II, which has put an end to its artificial postwar dependence on the United States and has confronted us with the necessity of determining how the Western community is to be organized, or, indeed, whether it is to be organized at all, now that it consists of two approximately equal centers of power and productivity in Europe and America. The real choice before the Western nations is not between American "hegemony" and European independence, but between an Atlantic partnership embracing all of the North Atlantic democracies and the division of the West into separate and competitive European and "Anglo-Saxon" communities. This is the central issue on which France and the United States are currently in disagreement.

My own belief, expressed many times in the past, is that the best hope for the North Atlantic democracies lies in the development, by gradual stages, of a close political, military, and economic partnership. The root of this belief is simple. Twice in this century the Western community has very nearly destroyed itself because of its profound internal conflicts. The two World Wars constituted a "civil war" of the West. As a result of these wars the democratic West lost its monopoly of power in the world, and some of its member nations barely survived as organized societies. It seems clear that if the Western community of nations is to survive and prosper, its prospects for doing so depend heavily on its success in overcoming its ancient animosities and uniting its member nations in a close working partnership for security and prosperity.

It makes little sense, under modern world conditions, to speak of Europe being independent of America or of America being independent of Europe. It is true that Europe has become far less dependent on the United States than it was fifteen years ago, in the sense that the threat of imminent catastrophe—of war and of political and economic collapse—has greatly receded. But in terms of continuing interests, of long-term security and stability, of the opportunity to realize our full economic potential and to improve the lives of our people, Europe and America remain profoundly dependent upon each other. Through a durable political and economic partnership, the West can disprove the Communist article of faith that capitalism must eventually succumb to its own internal rivalries and contradictions; in so doing, the West will undermine the very basis of communism's belief in the "inevitability" of its own universal triumph. In close partnership with each other, Western Europe and the United States have it within their power to attain greater security than they have known in this century, to help the underdeveloped countries overcome their ancient affliction of poverty, to bring unprecedented material well-being to their own people, and in so doing, to liberate them for the creative pursuits of civilized society.

It is inconceivable that France should be anything less than a leading participant in an Atlantic community. With her highly intelligent and educated people, her military power and her buoyant economy, and her great skill and experience in international relations, France is in a position to enrich and, quite possibly, to assure the success of a community of Atlantic democracies. France's partners are in need of her wisdom and her vision —the same wisdom which enabled President de Gaulle to end the Algerian war and to make France the guarantor of order and economic growth in large areas of Africa, and, indeed, in proportion to her resources, the leading nation of the free world in extending economic aid to underdeveloped countries. Many Frenchmen have feared that France cannot be herself as a participant in a larger community. They would do well to consider that the free world, of which France is an integral part, can have little chance of realizing the full measure of its hopes and opportunities without the participation of France.

At some time in the future, probably before the end of this decade, it will be necessary for the members of the Western Alliance to choose between "Gaullist" and "Atlantic" solutions to the problems of defense, economic relations, and the political organization of the West. On each of these issues there are now deep divisions between and within the member countries. These divisions are unfortunate but not fatal. They are, as I have suggested, the outgrowth of success rather than failure, of the fact that the Atlantic community now consists of two great power centers rather than only one. The West is militarily, politically, and economically strong, and its divisions pose no *immediate danger*. Their long-term significance, however, is very great, and it is important that we work patiently but vigorously for their resolution.

A great debate is under way both among and within the Atlantic nations. As long as it remains focused on the central issue, which is the security and prosperity of the West in the nuclear age, this debate can be constructive and cathartic rather than destructive and divisive. In America the discussion is now largely confined to government officials, writers, and scholars. It is to be hoped that the American people as a whole, who have devoted so much energy to an arid controversy about Cuba, will now divert some of their thoughts to the far more important issue of how the Atlantic democracies are to be organized for defense and prosperity.

The central issue of the debate is the defense of the West. President de Gaulle has made it plain that his defense policies, particularly with respect to the French nuclear force, are based on an assumption that the United States cannot be counted upon to meet its obligations for the defense of Europe. Because of the loss of the American nuclear monopoly and the acquisition by the Soviet Union of the power to devastate the American continent, the United States, in General de Gaulle's view, "is seeing its own survival as the principal objective in a possible conflict and is not considering the time, degree, terms, and conditions of its nuclear intervention for the defense of other regions, particularly Europe, except in relation to this natural and primary necessity."[2]

The assumption that the United States might stand aside while Europe is devastated and overrun is patently unfounded. In both word and deed, the United States has committed itself unalterably to the defense of Europe—by its adherence to

[2] Press Conference, July 29, 1963.

(98)

the NATO treaty, by innumerable declarations and reassurances, and by the presence in the heart of Europe of 400,000 American troops. I do not know what further assurances would be required to persuade General de Gaulle that we intend to honor our obligations.

But even if these commitments are set aside, it is inconceivable from a strategic point of view that the United States would stand aside—or that the Soviet Union would permit it to stand aside—while Western Europe was overrun. A third World War could not possibly follow the pattern of 1914 and 1939, in which France was attacked while the United States remained temporarily unscathed behind its ocean barriers. It is clearly understood in the United States that a successful Soviet attack on Europe would almost certainly be followed by an attack on the United States, and that even if it were not, the loss of Europe to the free world would leave the United States so weakened and isolated as to put its security, its economy, and probably its survival as a free society in the gravest jeopardy. Nor is it possible to imagine that the Russians would take the incredible risk of leaving the United States out of the conflict with its forces intact and able to intervene whenever it chose. If anything at all can be regarded as certain about a possible nuclear war, it is that the outcome of such a conflict would be determined, not in Western Europe, but in the two great centers of nuclear power, in Russia and the United States.

We are dealing here in possibilities, not certainties, but so is General de Gaulle. His strategic concept, as I see it, is one of preparing for the least likely contingency, that of a Communist attack on Western Europe from which the United States would be permitted and would choose to stand aside. It seems far more likely, if there is any rationality in Soviet strategic doctrine, that the reverse situation might occur—an assault on the United States from which Europe would be spared.

The overwhelming probability is that neither Europe nor America would be spared devastation in a nuclear war. In the two World Wars, the Western nations paid a grievous price for the illusion held by some of them that security could be found in isolation. We Americans have learned the costly lesson of our isolationism. It is our hope that our partners, who suffered far more grievously than we from the disunity of the past, will not be tempted to experiment with disunity again, because its price has become unacceptable and few would survive to profit from the lesson.

For these reasons it is essential that Europe, including France, commit itself to a unified defense of the West. Europe can and should make a far greater contribution to the Alliance than it is now making. The United States at present is putting 11 percent of its gross national product into defense and foreign aid, while some of its allies are doing less than half as much proportionately. The United States, which has committed itself to a unified defense of the West, will not of its volition abandon Europe, but this does not mean that it cannot be driven from Europe. If our partners pursue protectionist trade policies and decline to carry a proportion of the military and foreign aid burdens commensurate with their resources, the United States will be left with no choice but to reduce its commitments. General de Gaulle considers American withdrawal from Europe inevitable. It is not inevitable—unless Europe makes it so.

The necessary complement of a greater European contribution to the Alliance is greater European participation in the shaping and execution of its vital decisions. To a limited but not unimportant extent, this can be accomplished through a seaborne multilateral force, or, if preferred by the European allies, through their participation in the deployment and targeting of American land-based Minuteman missiles.

Beyond this, and probably more important, Europe can and should be brought into the strategic planning processes which govern the use of America's nuclear arsenal. A unified strategic planning system, aimed at the development of a strategic consensus among the allies, can be developed within the existing framework of NATO. The NATO Council, which has not played the significant role envisioned for it by the framers of the treaty in 1949, could now be developed into an allied strategic planning body on the model, say, of the combined Chiefs of Staff of World War II. It could become the allied forum for long-term political and military planning on the most fundamental questions of war and peace.

As Alastair Buchan, the Director of Britain's Institute for Strategic Studies, has pointed out, the beginning of a solution to the problem of command and control of nuclear weapons "lies in making the European allies partners in the Washington debate from which emerge policies on arms control, for the defense of Europe and for meeting the world-wide responsibilities of the United States. If the multilateral process is insufficient for all purposes, there are few people in Europe who would not welcome the deliberate cultivation of a 'special relationship' between France and the United States."[3]

Almost as important as the problem of the common defense is the challenge of shaping new economic relations among the Atlantic countries. Both the United States, through its Trade Expansion

[3] Alastair Buchan, "Partners and Allies," *Foreign Affairs*, July, 1963, p. 657.

Act of 1962, and the members of the European Economic Community, through their obligations under the Treaty of Rome, are committed to policies of expanded world trade. The progressive lowering of tariffs and other barriers to trade, starting with the "Kennedy round" of trade negotiations begun in the spring of 1964, would open the way to the development of an Atlantic trading community, which in turn could be expected to lead to new levels of economic prosperity and accelerated rates of economic growth in both Europe and America.

An Atlantic trading partnership is a conception based on the realities of mutual advantage and interest for both Europe and America. The United States, with a chronic deficit in its balance of payments, needs to participate in a large Atlantic trading area in order to expand its trade and its domestic economy and thus be able to finance its world-wide commitments, including its commitment to the defense of Europe. Should Europe become a closed, restrictive trading area, the United States would be increasingly hard pressed to meet its obligations.

The implications of protectionism are far more than commercial. Economic exclusiveness is also an instrument of political nationalism, posing barriers to co-operation in the political and military fields as well as trade. Conversely, the development of a thriving Atlantic trading community would have enormous political as well as economic implications for the entire free world. On the basis of a mutually beneficial trade relationship, both Europe and America can expand their capacity to deal effectively with the challenge of the Communist powers, to meet their obligations to the underdeveloped countries, and at the same time to give their own people a better and more abundant life.

Another area of Atlantic relations that can usefully engage our creative energies is that of devising institutions to perform specialized functions and also serve as symbols of the interdependence of the Western democracies. I do not think it feasible at present to establish Atlantic executive and judicial organs but I think there is merit in the proposal to create in the near future a consultative Atlantic Assembly to serve as a parliamentary body for both the North Atlantic Treaty Organization and the Organization for Economic Cooperation and Development. At its outset, and probably for some time thereafter, an Atlantic Assembly would probably be far more important as an institutional symbol of partnership than for its substantive contributions to the military work of NATO and the economic work of the OECD. Should such a body be created, the existing NATO Parliamentarians' Conference, which is an interparliamentary organization rather than a parliamentary body in its own right, and whose membership is of course confined to NATO countries, could and should be dissolved.

A major obstacle to the formation of an Atlantic Assembly is the reluctance of the European "neutrals" who are members of the OECD but not of NATO—that is to say, Sweden, Switzerland, Ireland, Austria, and Spain—to become involved in the affairs of the Western Military Alliance in any way. This difficulty, I believe, could be dealt with by dividing the work of an Atlantic parliamentary body between separate sessions or, if the neutrals prefer, between two separate assemblies, one responsible for military and political affairs pertaining to NATO, the other for social and economic affairs pertaining to the OECD.

Once the idea of an Atlantic parliamentary body is accepted, it seems to me that there need be no great difficulty about its mechanics. It would be feasible, for example, for the first three days of the annual meeting of the Assembly (or Assemblies) to be devoted to the consideration of military and political matters relating to NATO by appropriate committees, with only those delegates attending whose countries are members of NATO. The fourth day might be devoted to a plenary session at which reports of these committees would be considered and acted upon, again with only NATO delegates attending. At this point, those members of the Assembly whose countries are not members of NATO (or, if a dual system should be adopted, the neutrals who belong only to the second Assembly) would join the conference. The next three days, perhaps following a week end between the two separate parts of the conference, would be devoted to the consideration of economic and scientific matters by the appropriate committees with all delegates attending. There would then follow a second plenary session at which reports on these matters would be considered and acted upon, again with all delegates attending. This scheme is purely illustrative; it is meant only to suggest that the mechanics of the Atlantic Assembly pose no insuperable problem. The essential requirement is a general political commitment to some arrangement which, without compromising the neutrality of the neutrals, will bring most or all of the Atlantic countries together in an Atlantic parliamentary organization.

The powers and functions of a consultative Atlantic Assembly would have to be thoroughly considered by the parliamentarians of the Atlantic nations. At the minimum, however, the Assembly should have the following powers: the right to have regular reports from NATO and OECD; the right to submit questions and receive either answers or formal refusals to answer from the Councils and Secretaries General of these two organizations; the right to invite representatives of the Councils and the Secretariats of NATO and OECD to appear before the Assembly or its appropriate committees for questioning, and to have such invitations either accepted or formally refused; the right to submit recommendations to the two organizations, and after a proper interval of time require reports on actions taken or not taken as a result of the Assembly's recommendations. In addition, it might be worth considering whether the Assembly should be empowered, by simple majority or perhaps by a two-thirds vote, to express its confidence or lack of confidence in specific actions or decisions of the two executive bodies. An Assembly vested with such authority would of course be under an obligation to exercise restraint and self-discipline in its requests and recommendations, confining the latter to clear, specific, and practical proposals.

The creation of a consultative Atlantic Assembly would constitute an important political step, and an even more important psychological step, in a renewal of the movement toward Atlantic partnership. The contribution of such a body would for some time perhaps be more symbolic than substantive, but symbols are a vital part of political creativity and the *potential* substantive contribution of an Atlantic Assembly is considerable. The establishment of an Atlantic parliamentary body would not solve the problem of Western unity, but it would constitute at least a partial reversal of direction from the baleful tendencies of the recent past, and might thus set the Atlantic nations back on the course of unity, giving new life to the most promising trend in the modern history of the West.

A new idea has sprung up out of the ashes of two World Wars: the idea that the sovereign nation can no longer serve as the ultimate unit of personal loyalty and responsibility. We have begun to perceive that our happiness and prosperity, and perhaps even our survival, may depend on whether we allow the West to succumb once again to divisive and destructive nationalism, or whether, through policies of partnership, we make the West so strong that no one will dare attack it and so prosperous and progressive that it will serve as a model and a magnet for the entire world. We have begun to perceive that the frontiers of freedom are wider than the frontiers of Europe or America, and that if we are to create a world environment in which free societies can survive and flourish, we must do so as partners in a community of free nations.

"Great ideas come into the world as gently as doves," wrote Albert Camus. "Perhaps then, if we listen attentively, we shall hear, amid the uproar of empires and nations, a faint flutter of wings, the gentle stirring of life and hope."

IV

The Cold War in American Life

The Constitution of the United States, in the words of its preamble, was established, among other reasons, in order to "provide for the common defense, promote the general welfare, and secure the blessings of liberty. . . ." In the past generation the emphasis of our public policy has been heavily weighted on measures for the common defense to the considerable neglect of programs for promoting the liberty and welfare of our people. The reason for this, of course, has been the exacting demands of two World Wars and an intractable cold war, which have wrought vast changes in the character of American life.

Of all the changes in American life wrought by the cold war, the most important by far, in my opinion, has been the massive diversion of energy and resources from the creative pursuits of civilized society to the conduct of a costly and interminable struggle for world power. We have been compelled, or have felt ourselves compelled, to reverse the traditional order of our national priorities, relegating individual and community life to places on the scale below the enormously expensive military and space activities that constitute our program of national security. Thus, we work ourselves into a fearful state of alarm over every incident on the Berlin access routes while blandly ignoring the increase of crime and violence in our great cities; we regard ourselves as gravely threatened by the rantings of a Cuban demagogue while taking little notice of the social disintegration caused by chronic unemployment; we undertake a $20-billion crash program to be first on the moon in order to avoid a possible blow to our pride while refusing to spend even a fraction of that amount for urgently needed federal aid to public education.

These of course are not the only effects of the continued world crisis on American life. There have been many others, some most welcome and constructive. Directly or indirectly, the world struggle with communism has stimulated economic and industrial expansion, accelerated the pace of intellectual inquiry and scientific discovery, broken the shell of American isolation, and greatly increased public knowledge and awareness of the world outside the United States. At the same time, the continuing world conflict has cast a shadow on the tone of American life by introducing a strand of apprehension and tension into a national style which has traditionally been one of buoyant optimism. The continuing and inconclusive struggle, new in American experience, has, in Walt Rostow's words, "imposed a sense of limitation on the nation's old image of itself, a limitation which has been accepted with greater or less maturity and which has touched the nation's domestic life at many points with elements of escapism, with a tendency to search for scapegoats, with simple worry, and with much thoughtful, responsive effort as well."[1]

Overriding all these changes, however, good and bad, has been the massive diversion of wealth and talent from individual and community life for the increasingly complex and costly effort of maintaining a minimum level of national security in a world in which no nation can be immune from the threat

[1] W. W. Rostow, *The United States in the World Arena* (New York: Harper & Row, Publishers, Inc., 1960), p. 451.

of sudden catastrophe. We have had to turn away from our hopes in order to concentrate on our fears, and the result has been accumulating neglect of those things which bring happiness and beauty and fulfillment into our lives. The "public happiness," in August Heckscher's term, has become a luxury to be postponed to some distant day when the dangers that now beset us will have disappeared.

This inversion of priorities, I think, is the real meaning of the cold war in American life. It has consumed money and time and talent that could otherwise have been used to build schools and homes and hospitals, to remove the blight of ugliness that is spreading over the cities and highways of America, and to overcome the poverty and hopelessness that afflict the lives of one-fifth of the people in an otherwise affluent society. It has put a high premium on avoiding innovation at home, because new programs involve controversy as well as expense and it is felt that we cannot afford domestic divisions at a time when external challenges require us to maintain the highest possible degree of national unity. Far more pervasively than the United Nations or the Atlantic community could ever do, the cold war has encroached upon our sovereignty; it has given the Russians the major voice in determining what proportion of our federal budget must be allocated to the military and what proportion, therefore, cannot be made available for domestic social and economic projects. This is the price that we have been paying for the cold war, and it has been a high price indeed.

At least as striking as the inversion of priorities which the cold war has enforced upon American life is the apparent readiness with which the American people have consented to defer programs for their welfare and happiness in favor of costly military and space programs. Indeed, if the Congress accurately reflects the temper of the country, then the American people are not only willing, they are eager, to sacrifice education and urban renewal and public health programs—to say nothing of foreign aid—to the requirements of the armed forces and the space agency. There is indeed a most striking paradox in the fact that military budgets of more than $50 billion are adopted by the Congress afer only perfunctory debate, while domestic education and welfare programs involving sums which are mere fractions of the military budget are painstakingly examined and then either considerably reduced or rejected outright. I sometimes suspect that in its zeal for armaments at the expense of education and welfare, the Congress tends to overrepresent those of our citizens who are extraordinarily agitated about national security and extraordinarily vigorous about making their agitation known.

(113)

It may be that the people and their representatives are making a carefully reasoned sacrifice of welfare to security. It may be, but I doubt it. The sacrifice is made so eagerly as to cause one to suspect that it is fairly painless, that indeed the American people prefer military rockets to public schools, and flights to the moon to urban renewal. In a perverse way, we have grown rather attached to the cold war. It occupies us with a seemingly clear and simple challenge from outside and diverts us from problems here at home which many Americans would rather not try to solve, some because they are genuinely and deeply preoccupied with foreign affairs, others because they find domestic problems tedious and pedestrian, others because they genuinely believe these problems to be personal rather than public, others because they are unwilling to be drawn into an abrasive national debate as to whether poverty, unemployment, and inadequate education are in fact national rather than local or individual concerns.

We have been preoccupied with foreign affairs for twenty-five years, and while striking progress has nonetheless been made in certain areas of our domestic life, the overall agenda of neglect has grown steadily longer. We can no longer afford to defer problems of slums and crime and poverty and inadequate education. In the long run, the solution of these problems has as vital a bearing on the success of our foreign policies as on the public happiness at home. We must therefore re-assess the priorities of our public policy, with a view to redressing the disproportion between our military and space efforts on the one hand, and our education and human welfare programs on the other. We must overcome the "cold war" mentality that has persuaded millions of sensible and intelligent citizens that the prosecution of the cold war is our only truly essential national responsibility, that missiles and nuclear armaments and space flights are so vital to the safety of the nation that it is almost unpatriotic to question their cost and their proliferation, and that in the face of these necessities the internal requirements of the country, with respect to its schools and cities and public services, must be left for action at some remote time in the future—as if these requirements were not themselves vital to the national security, and as if, indeed, our generation is likely to know more tranquil days.

In the 1830s Alexis de Tocqueville saw America as a nation with a passion for peace, one in which the "principle of equality," which made it possible for a man to improve his status rapidly in civilian life, made it most unlikely that many Americans would ever be drawn to form a professional military caste. In 1961, President Eisenhower warned the nation of the pervasive and growing power of a "military-industrial complex." Tocqueville was quite right in his judgment that the United States was unlikely to become a *militarist* society. We have, however, as a result of world-wide involvements and responsibilities, become a great *military* power, with a vast military establishment that absorbs over half of our federal budget, profoundly influences the nation's economy, and exercises a gradually expanding influence on public attitudes and policies.

Without becoming militarist in the sense of committing themselves to the military virtues as standards of personal behavior, the American people have nonetheless come to place great—and, in my opinion, excessive—faith in military solutions to political problems. Many Americans have come to regard our defense establishment as the heart and soul of our foreign policy, rather than as one of a number of instruments of foreign policy whose effectiveness depends, not only on its size and variety, but also on the skill, and restraint, with which it is used.

Our faith in the military is akin to our faith in technology. We are a people more comfortable with machines than with intellectual abstractions. The military establishment is a vast and enormously complex machine, a tribute to the technological genius of the American people; foreign policy is an abstract and esoteric art, widely regarded as a highly specialized occupation of "eastern intellectuals," but not truly an "American" occupation. Our easy reliance on the military establishment as the foundation of our foreign policy is not unlike the reliance which we place on automobiles, televisions, and refrigerators: they work in a predictable and controllable manner, and on the rare occasions when they break down, any good mechanic can put them back in working order.

The trouble with the American technological bias is that it can conceal but not eliminate the ultimate importance of human judgment. Like any other piece of machinery, our military establishment can be no better than the judgment of those who control it. In a democracy, control is intended to be exercised by the people and their elected representatives. To a very considerable extent the American people are not now exercising effective control over the armed forces; nor indeed is the Congress, despite its Constitutional responsibilities in this field. Partly because of anxieties about the cold war, partly because of our natural technological bias, which leads us to place extraordinary faith in the ability of "technicians" to deal with matters that we ourselves find incomprehensible, and partly because of the vested interests of the "military-industrial complex," we are permitting the vast military establishment largely to run itself, to determine its own needs, and to tell us what sacrifices are expected of us to sustain the national arsenal of weapons.

David Lloyd George once declared that "there is no greater fatuity than a political judgment dressed in a military uniform." To the extent that the American people and the Congress shrink from questioning the size and cost of our defense establishment, they are permitting military men, with their highly specialized viewpoints, to make political judgments of the greatest importance regarding the priorities of public policy and the allocation of public funds.

The abnegation of responsibility by the Congress in this field is strikingly illustrated by its debates— or, more accurately, "nondebates"—on the defense budget. When, for example, Senator McGovern of South Dakota suggested in September, 1963, that defense spending might be reduced by 5 percent, the Senate, with virtually no discussion, voted the McGovern amendment down by a vote of 70 to 2 and proceeded, after an afternoon of desultory discussion, to enact the whole defense appropriation bill. When later that fall I had the dubious honor of managing the foreign aid bill on the Senate floor through three weeks of extremely contentious debate, I could not help noting how astonishingly the forces of "economy" had picked up strength between the debate on the $50-billion defense appropriation and the $4-billion foreign aid bill.

The Congress has, in recent years, speeded the enactment of the defense budget with much less than the customary concern as to its size and content—except, on occasion, when a special opportunity arises to give, or force upon, the executive branch more than it has requested. In 1964, for example, both Houses enacted a military procurement authorization bill of more than $17 billion within less than two months of the opening of the Congressional session. The only controversial item in the bill was an amendment authorizing $52 million for development of a new strategic manned bomber, which was adopted by both Houses despite the firm opposition of the Secretary of Defense. In the course of this debate, Senator Nelson of Wisconsin posed a most pertinent question. "I am questioning," he said, "what is apparently an established tradition—perhaps a national attitude —which holds that a bill to spend billions of dollars for the machinery of war must be rushed through the House and the Senate in a matter of hours, while a treaty to advance the cause of peace, or a program to help the underdeveloped nations of the world, or a bill to guarantee the rights of all our citizens, or a bill to advance the interests of the poor, must be scrutinized and debated and amended and thrashed over for weeks and perhaps months."[2]

"Like most other Americans . . . ," writes Julius Duscha of the *Washington Post,* "Members of Congress believe that the bigger the defense budget, the safer the country. And in today's world there is no question that the United States must spend billions to keep up its defenses. But record-breaking budgets year after year do not necessarily mean a stronger nation. The bigger any government program gets, the greater are the dangers that funds will be wasted and that the goals of the program will become entangled in a morass of vested interests, venal political considerations, and the rivalries that inevitably evolve from them. And there is no better catharsis for huge government expenditures than informed, skeptical, and continued questioning of them."[3]

The ease with which defense budgets are enacted by Congress is due in no small degree to the enormous importance of defense spending for the economy. Defense contractors and great numbers of workers all over the country have a vested interest in a high level of defense spending. It is

[2] *Congressional Record,* February 26, 1964, p. 3584.
[3] Julius Duscha, "Arms and the Big Money Men," *Harper's,* March, 1964, p. 40.

the beneficiaries of the jobs and profits that defense spending creates, along with the generals and admirals, who constitute the formidable "military-industrial complex." And because of the jobs and profits stimulated by defense, Members of Congress have taken a benign attitude toward waste and duplication in the defense budget that is nothing less than amazing by contrast with the deeply held convictions about economy that influence their attitude toward education, urban renewal, or foreign aid.

The truly astonishing thing about the uncritical support which the American people and their representatives give the military establishment is the apparent enthusiasm with which the sacrifice of personal and community interests is made. Goldsworthy Lowes Dickinson was, if anything, understating the matter when he wrote that "Nations are quite capable of starving every other side of life—education, sanitation, housing, public health, everything that contributes to life, physical, intellectual, moral, and spiritual—in order to maintain their armaments."[4]

The uncritical acceptance of astronomical military expenditures by millions of Americans is matched by a similar extravagance with respect to

[4] Goldsworthy Lowes Dickinson, *The Choice Before Us* (London: George Allen & Unwin, 1917), pp. 200-201.

space flights, and particularly the project for landing an American on the moon by 1970, at a cost of something between $20 and $30 billion.

As with our defense program, the problem of space expenditures is one of priorities. The benefits of space exploration may indeed be considerable, but they are remote and incalculable. The need for schools and jobs is immediate and pressing. The space program, we are told, is important for our security and prestige. This is perhaps true, but the education of our people and the growth of our economy are far more important because these are the foundations of national power. To allow them to deteriorate is to undermine our national security as surely as would the dismantling of our military power.

The question is not whether we should or should not send a manned rocket ship to the moon, but whether the project is so vital and so urgent as to warrant the indefinite postponement of other national efforts. This question has been debated at length, both in the Congress and in various publications. I have heard nothing to persuade me that it would be a national calamity if the landing on the moon were delayed until 1980 or 1990. I have heard and seen a great deal which persuades me that our continuing neglect of deteriorating schools and rising unemployment *would* be a national calamity.

The argument most frequently heard in support of Project Apollo, the moon shot program, is that if we do not pursue a crash program in space the Russians will get to the moon ahead of us. This argument can be challenged on two grounds: first, it is not at all clear that the Russians are *trying* to beat us to the moon; secondly—and more important—it is even less clear that it would be an irretrievable disaster if they did.

Sir Bernard Lovell, Director of the Jodrell Bank Observatory in Britain, reported, after a visit to Soviet space observatories in July, 1963, that he saw no evidence of a high priority manned moon program. Sir Bernard was told by Russian scientists that they saw insuperable economic and technical problems to landing a man on the moon, and that in any case they believed they could get nearly all the information they wanted by a "soft" landing of instruments on the moon. "I think, at the moment," said Sir Bernard, "the Americans are racing themselves concerning moon research."

But what if the Russians really are committed to a race to the moon? What if they do get there first? Would that be an unmitigated disaster and disgrace for America? Would it make us a second-rate people, shamed in the eyes of the world and in our own eyes as well? I do not think so. I think it would be a temporary embarrassment and annoyance, but not a calamity. It would hurt our pride but not our lives as free men in a free society. Most emphatically, it would not change the course of history.

The issue between freedom and dictatorship is a great deal more than a competition in technological stunts. The real competition is between two conflicting concepts of man and of his life in organized societies. Does it not follow that our success has a great deal to do with our capacity to employ and educate our people to create the conditions for human happiness and individual fulfillment in a free society? If, at the end of this decade, the Russians should have reached the moon and we should not, but have instead succeeded in building the best system of public education in the world, in the renovation of our cities and transport, in the virtual elimination of slums and crime, in the alleviation of poverty and disease, whose prestige would be higher, who would then be ahead in the world-wide struggle for the minds of men?

In reflecting on the crash program to reach the moon, and the irrational priorities of public policy which it involves, I am reminded of the passage in Jonathan Swift's *Gulliver's Travels* in which the "author" visits the Academy of Projectors in Lagado. The Academy is an institution in which scientists engage in studies and experiments of brilliant inventiveness, which, however, are gro-

tesquely irrelevant to the needs of the destitute
society in which they live. One scientist is engaged
in a project for extracting sunbeams out of cucum-
bers, to be put in hermetically sealed vials and let
out to warm the air in raw and rainy summers.
Another has devised a method for building houses
from the roof downward to the foundations, and
another has invented a contrivance by which "the
most ignorant person would be able to write books
of philosophy, poetry, politics, law, mathematics,
and theology without having to study."

The Academy of Lagado, and others like it, Swift
explains, had become great centers of scientific
progress and invention. The only drawback of the
great preoccupation with science is that "in the
meantime, the whole country lies in waste, the
houses are in ruins, and the people are without
food and clothes." But far from being discouraged,
the people are enormously enthusiastic about the
academies and their work, and the few troglodytes
who persist in living in neat houses and raising
edible crops are "looked on with contempt as
enemies of art, who preferred their own ease and
comfort to the general improvement of the country."

It is frequently said that we did not provide
adequate funds for education and other vital
domestic needs before we had a space program
and that there is no assurance that we would in-

crease our efforts in these areas if the space program were abandoned or reduced. This, I am bound to concede, may well be true, although the Congress has come close several times to adopting a meaningful general program of federal aid to education, and it is possible that the reduction of our space expenditures would provide the impetus for the enactment of a general education bill. In any case, I see little merit in the view that since we will not spend money anyway on things we urgently need, we might as well spend it on things we do not need. If it comes to that, I for one would rather not spend the money at all.

Perhaps more important than the costs of space research is the fact that it is drawing urgently needed scientific talent away from the civilian economy. From 1954 to 1963, for example, the number of research and development scientists and engineers in industry increased by about 160,000, and all but 30,000 of these were drawn into government-sponsored projects.

There is a real danger that our national programs in defense and space will become a drain on the civilian economy and will jeopardize our position in world trade. At present only 25 percent of our total national research and development spending are going into industrial research for civilian purposes. Western European countries are spending twice as large a proportion of their gross national products as the United States for civilian research and development. The Japanese, largely as a result of progress through civilian research, have introduced the first transistorized television sets into the United States, are getting twice our rate of production from textile machinery, and are turning out automated ships that can carry more cargo than our ships with smaller crews.

Equally alarming is the prospective diversion of scientists and engineers from careers in university teaching. In the next decade there will be a great increase in our college population. If the present teacher-student ratio is to be maintained, the universities in the next several years will have to retain two thirds of their current output of new Ph.D.s instead of the present one third. Thus, the current flow of graduate research scholars to government and industry would have to be cut in half. It is just at this critical point that the demand for scientific talent for the space program is rapidly rising. It is increasingly clear that the supply of scientists and engineers in the present decade will not be sufficient to meet the demands of a mushrooming space program, a rapidly expanding college population, and all the other needs of the civilian economy.

These are only some of the compelling reasons for bringing our space program into a more realistic relationship to pressing national needs. In the face of all the unsolved problems of our country—problems of inadequate education, racial tensions, rising unemployment, of urban blight and rising crime—I cannot bring myself to believe that landing an American on the moon represents the most urgent need, the most compelling challenge, or the most promising opportunity before the American people in this decade.

Many Americans may regard huge military and space programs as the only truly urgent requirements on our national agenda, but it is difficult to believe that this enthusiasm is shared by the 4.2 million Americans who are unemployed or by the 30 million Americans who have incomes of less than $3,000 a year.

While the cold war and our enormously costly national security programs pre-empt so much of our time and attention and national wealth, the most important resources of our country—its human resources—are being extravagantly wasted and neglected. As the President's *Manpower Report,* issued early in 1964, points out, unemployment in 1963 increased to 5.7 percent of the labor force despite major advances in production and employment; unemployment of young workers, between the ages of 16 and 19, reached 17 percent in 1963 while unemployment among nonwhite Americans stood at 11 percent; despite an unemployment rate twice as high for school dropouts as for high-school graduates, 30 percent of all young people continue to end their education before completing high school; despite the decline in unskilled jobs and the expanding demand for professional, technical, clerical, and service workers—for workers, that is, with at least high-school education and specialized training—nearly a million young people are leaving school every year without having completed elementary or secondary school.

These are only a few of the statistics of hopelessness and deprivation that afflict the lives of millions of Americans. Unless the present trend is reversed, 7.5 million of the 26 million young people between 16 and 24 who will enter the labor force during the present decade will be school dropouts. These undereducated young men and women are for the most part the children of poverty. The basic fact to be contended with, as President Johnson pointed out in his message to Congress of March, 1964, on poverty, is that "There are millions of Americans—one fifth of our people—who have not shared in the abundance which has been granted to most of us, and on whom the gates of opportunity have been closed." It is one of the tragedies, and one of the great failures, of our national life that in the years between 1936 and 1964, while the total wealth and productivity of the nation grew tremendously, the number of ill-housed, ill-clothed,

and ill-fed Americans dropped only from one third
to one fifth of our population.

The statistics of poverty, though striking, are
antiseptic compared to the actual misery and hopelessness of being poor. The real meaning of poverty
is not just loss of learning and productivity, but
thousands of angry and dispossessed teen-agers
who make our city streets dangerous for "respectable" citizens; 350,000 youngsters across the nation
who form what the Secretary of Labor has de-
scribed as an "outlaw pack," because they have
stopped looking for work, are unemployed today,
and will remain so for the rest of their lives; children in a blighted mining town in eastern Ken-
tucky who are potbellied and anemic from lack of
food; share-croppers, white as well as black, living
in squalid shacks and working for a few dollars a
day—when they can find work at all—anywhere
in a crescent of rural poverty that extends from
Virginia southward across Georgia and Alabama
into the Mississippi delta and the Ozarks.

Poverty in America has a racially different moral
connotation from poverty in underdeveloped nations. The poor countries of the world have the ex-
cuse, for what it is worth, that the means of feed-
ing, housing, and educating their people simply do
not exist. In America the means do exist; the
failure is essentially one of distribution. The children who go to bed hungry in a Harlem slum or

a West Virginia mining town are not being deprived because no food can be found to give them; they are going to bed hungry because, despite all our miracles of invention and production, we have not yet found a way to make the necessities of life available to all of our citizens—including those whose failure is not a lack of personal industry or initiative, but only an unwise choice of parents.

What is to be done? In his poverty message to the Congress, the President made proposals for a constructive start—although only a start—toward meeting the problem of poverty in America. Under the proposed Economic Opportunity Act, a National Job Corps would undertake the social rehabilitation, through basic education, job training, and work experience, of 100,000 young men "whose background, health, and education makes them least fit for useful work"; a work-training program would provide vocational education and part-time jobs for 200,000 young men and women in projects to be developed by state and local governments and nonprofit agencies; a national work-study program would provide federal funds for part-time jobs for 140,000 young Americans who, though qualified, would otherwise be unable to afford to go to college. In addition, the President's program would encourage and help finance local antipoverty programs, would enlist volunteers in the war against poverty, and would undertake other finan-

cial and educational programs, all to be co-ordinated under a new Office of Economic Opportunity.

President Johnson's program can serve as a point
of departure for a full-scale national program to
eliminate poverty and unemployment from American life. Such a program must be mounted through
government fiscal policy, public works, and expansive economic policies, but primarily through
programs of education and training. Education is
not the whole solution, but it is, by all available
evidence, the keystone of the arch. As John
Kenneth Galbraith has written, "To the best of
knowledge there is no place in the world where a
well-educated population is really poor."[5]

Building on this premise, Professor Galbraith
has proposed that the hundred lowest income communities in the country be designated "special educational districts," to be equipped with primary
and secondary schools and recreational and trans-
portation facilities of the highest quality. The
schools would be staffed by an elite corps of highly
qualified, highly trained, and *well-paid* teachers.
Grants would be provided for food and clothing
for the pupils when needed, as well as counseling
and medical and psychiatric services. After one
year the program would be extended to another

[5] John Kenneth Galbraith, "Let Us Begin: An Invitation to
Action on Poverty," *Harper's*, March, 1964, p. 26.

150 or 200 areas and eventually would be extended to cover all areas of great need. As income rises in the recipient school districts, the schools would be turned back to the localities.[6]

The Galbraith plan is an excellent one, and I, for one, would welcome the submission of such a plan to the Congress, although there can be no doubt that it would generate great controversy. I think that we must face up to the need for major new legislation in the field of education regardless of the partisan divisions which it may provoke. We must do so if we truly mean to alleviate the scourge of poverty in American life. And although it is clear that there is no simple dollar-for-dollar relationship between savings in the defense and space budgets and Congressional willingness to appropriate money for education, it seems to me quite possible that the elimination of superfluous defense and space expenditures would help overcome the reluctance to support education legislation of certain Members of Congress whose concern with economy is genuine and strong.

As a result of the rapidly spreading automation of the American economy, the traditional mechanism of distributing purchasing power through employment and income is breaking down. In essence, our ability to generate economic demands is falling steadily behind our ability to increase the

[6] *Ibid.*

supply of purchasable goods and services. It may be that the growing disequilibrium is so profound as to be irreversible by government policies in support of education, economic growth, and full employment. If so, we shall eventually have to devise new ways of providing income to those who cannot be put to gainful work.

Whether truly radical measures will be required or not, there is no question that if our national war on poverty is to come anywhere near the goal of "total victory" proclaimed by President Johnson, it will require enormous public effort and a great deal of public money. To those who shrink from such a commitment in the name of economy, I would emphasize that the elimination of poverty and the improvement of education are at least as important to the security of our country in the long run as the maintenance of a strong defense establishment, and a good deal more important than a voyage to the moon. I commend to them the words of Edmund Burke, that "Economy is a distributive virtue, and consists not in saving but in selection. Parsimony requires no providence, no sagacity, no powers of combination, no comparison, no judgment."[7]

These questions of education, employment, and poverty have a profound bearing on the Negro

[7] Edmund Burke, *Letter to a Noble Lord* (1796).

movement for equal rights and opportunity. They are in fact the heart and core of the civil-rights issue, which, far from being a separate and distinct national problem, is bound up with these broader problems both in its causes and in its prospective resolution. ". . . the Negro," writes Joseph P. Lyford, an executive of the Center for the Study of Democratic Institutions and former staff director for New York City's Public Education Association, "has done a great deal more than expose the contradictions between the actual and professed beliefs of the American citizen. His battle for freedom has established the fact that the Negro cannot win equality of opportunity until American society as a whole develops some way of dealing with the rise of mass unemployment and the growing ineffectiveness of our political and educational system. What we call the 'Negro revolution' is a preview of a much bigger crisis to come; it is forcing us to take a closer look at certain extremely unpleasant developments that are going to transform or destroy the traditional institutions and habits of all of us, black and white."[8]

It seems clear that even the strongest civil-rights legislation can have only a marginal effect in advancing the hopes of the Negro for a fair and decent status in American society. Unaccompanied

[8] Joseph P. Lyford, "Proposal for a Revolution—Part 1," *The Saturday Review,* October 19, 1963, p. 19.

by major national efforts in the fields of education and employment, civil-rights legislation can have little more than symbolic value. At most, it can vindicate a principle without significantly alleviating the *conditions* of poverty and undereducation which are the core of the problem.

If there is a solution to the problem of racial discrimination in our society—and I believe there is—it lies in a direct assault on the national conditions which foster and sustain it. These conditions are poverty, unemployment, and inadequate education. The entry of a pair of Negro children into an all-white school in Birmingham may vindicate a principle, but it has little bearing on the needs of millions of children all over the nation, white as well as Negro, who are being denied adequate education in overcrowded schools staffed by inadequate numbers of underpaid and undertrained teachers. Forcing open a construction union in New York to a few Negro apprentices may be regarded as a victory for equal opportunity, but, as Mr. Lyford writes, "it has almost no bearing on the employment prospects of hundreds of thousands of teen-agers and millions of adults—white and Negro—who are sinking to the bottom of a society that may very well have 14 million unemployed by 1970."[9]

Despite notable advances in the formal rights

[9] *Ibid.*, p. 29.

of Negroes since the Supreme Court decision of 1954, employment prospects for Negroes are actually declining, and declining at an accelerating rate. The causes of this are inadequate education and the spread of automation. Factory and service jobs, which have been the principal source of Negro employment, are being eliminated by automation at rates estimated to be anywhere from 17,000 to 40,000 a week.

The point which I wish to emphasize is that the overriding economic and social problems of America—poverty, race relations, unemployment, and defective education—are profoundly related to each other and to our position in the world as well, and that there can be no resolution of any one of these problems in the absence of a national effort to resolve all of them.

The time for such an effort is long overdue. We have allowed these problems to fester and grow during the long years of our preoccupation with crises and challenges abroad. To neglect them further is not to accept conditions as they now exist, but to acquiesce in the slow but relentless disintegration of our free society. The cold war, as David Riesman has written, "is a distraction from serious thought about man's condition on the planet."[10] My own belief is that the prevailing con-

[10] David Riesman, *Abundance for What?* (Garden City, N.Y.: Doubleday, 1964), p. 98.

ditions of our foreign relations are favorable to a refocusing of our efforts on problems here at home, but even if they are not, it would still be essential to revise our priorities, because the success of our foreign policy depends ultimately on the strength and character of our society, which in turn depend on our success in resolving the great social and economic issues of American life.

Of all the requirements on our national agenda, none warrants higher priority than the need to turn some part of our thoughts and our creative energies away from the cold war back in on America itself. If we do so, and if we sustain the effort, we may find that the most vital assets of our nation, for its public happiness and its security as well, remain locked within our own frontiers, in our cities and in our countryside, in our work and in our leisure, in the hearts and minds of our people.

V

Conclusion

Of all the myths that have troubled the lives of modern nations the most pervading have been those associated with the nation itself. Nationalism, which is pre-eminently a state of mind rather than a state of nature, has become a dominant and universal state of mind in the twentieth century.[1] Designating the sovereign nation-state as the ultimate object of individual loyalty and obliga-

[1] *See* Hans Kohn, *The Idea of Nationalism* (New York: Macmillan, 1944).

tion, the idea of nationalism prevails in every region of the world, in rich nations as well as poor nations, in democracies as well as dictatorships. Nationalism, I believe, is the most powerful single force in the world politics of the twentieth century, more powerful than communism or democracy or any other system of ideas about social organization.

It is also the most dangerous. Dividing communities against one another, it has become a universal force at precisely the time in history when technology has made the world a single unit in the physical sense—interdependent for economic, political, and cultural purposes and profoundly interdependent for survival in the nuclear age. Having for many centuries represented a broadening of human loyalties from their family and tribal origins—as indeed it does even today in certain African countries which are still emerging from tribalism—the nation has now become a barrier to the historical process by which men have associated themselves in ever larger political and economic communities. In the face of a compelling need for broader associations, nationalism sets both great and small nations against one another, to their vast peril and at an enormous price in the welfare and happiness of their people.

"How," asked a seventeenth-century French historian, "does it serve the people and add to their happiness if their ruler extend his empire by annexing the provinces of his enemies; . . . how does it help me or my countrymen that my sovereign be successful and covered with glory, that my country be powerful and dreaded, if, sad and worried, I live in oppression and poverty?"[2]

The question, phrased somewhat differently, is how and why it happens that the groups into which men organize themselves come to be regarded as ends in themselves, as living organisms with needs and preferences of their own which are separate from and superior to those of individuals, warranting, when necessary, the sacrifice of the hopes and pleasures of individual men. One of the paradoxes of politics is that so great a part of our organized efforts as societies is directed toward abstract and mystic goals—toward spreading a faith or ideology, toward enhancing the pride and power and self-respect of the nation, as if the nation had a "self" and a "soul" apart from the individuals who compose it, and as if the wishes of individual men, for life and happiness and prosperity, were selfish and dishonorable and unworthy of our best creative efforts.

Throughout history men have contested causes that had little to do with their own needs and

[2] Jean de la Bruyère, *"Du Souverain ou de la République,"* in *Oeuvres Complètes,* Julian Benda, Ed., Bibliothèque de la Pléiade (Paris: Librairie Gallimard, 1951), Vol. 23, pp. 302-303.

preferences, but until quite recently this tendency, though irrational, has been less than irreparably destructive. Since the invention of nuclear weapons, it has become possible that the great struggles of international politics will bring about the destruction not merely of cities and nations but of much or all of human civilization. This great change has made international politics dangerous as it has never been before, confronting us with the need to ask ourselves whether there are not other causes to be served than the struggle for prestige and power, causes which are closer to human needs and far less likely to lead to nuclear incineration.

Science has radically changed the conditions of human life on earth. It has expanded our knowledge and our power but not our capacity to use them with wisdom. Somehow, if we are to save ourselves, we must find this capacity. We must find in ourselves the judgment and the will to alter the focus of international politics in ways which are at once less dangerous to mankind and more beneficial to individual men. Without deceiving ourselves as to the difficulty of the task, we must try to develop a new capacity for creative political action.

"If to do were as easy as to know what were good to do," wrote Shakespeare, "chapels had been churches, and poor men's cottages princes' palaces."[3] The task of altering the character of international politics is of course infinitely more difficult than acknowledging the need to do so, and that is difficult enough. But if we are very clear about the difficulties of change, about how change occurs in human affairs and how it does not occur, then perhaps we can begin to alter the passions and prejudices that lead nations into wars as well as the weapons with which they fight them. We must recognize, first of all, that the ultimate source of war and peace lies in human nature and that nothing is more difficult to change than the human mind. "Even given the freest scope by their institutions," wrote Ruth Benedict, "men are never inventive enough to make more than minute changes. From the point of view of an outsider the most radical innovations in any culture amount to no more than a minor revision."[4]

To recognize the difficulty of change is to recognize its possibility as well. Those who are sanguine about the power of reason to reshape human attitudes are soon disillusioned and driven to a pessimism which is no less erroneous than the false optimism with which they began. The beginning of wisdom, I think, is to understand that, difficult as it is, it is yet possible to alter human attitudes,

[3] Portia in *The Merchant of Venice*, Act I, Scene ii.
[4] Ruth Benedict, *Patterns of Culture* (New York: Penguin Books, 1946), p. 76.

and that to do so, to however slight a degree, is to shape the course of human events.

Some years ago a group of eight distinguished psychologists and social scientists issued a statement on the causes of nationalistic aggression and the conditions necessary for international understanding. They stated in part:

"To the best of our knowledge, there is no evidence to indicate that wars are necessary and inevitable consequences of 'human nature' as such. While men vary greatly in their capacities and temperaments, we believe there are vital needs common to all men which must be fulfilled in order to establish and maintain peace: men everywhere want to be free from hunger and disease, from insecurity and fear; men everywhere want fellowship and the respect of their fellow men; the chance for personal growth and development."[5]

If conflict and war are not indigenous to our nature, why, we may ask, are they so prevalent? "The crux of the matter," writes social psychologist Gordon Allport, "lies in the fact that while most people deplore war, they nonetheless *expect* it to continue. *And what people expect determines their behavior.* . . . the indispensable condition of war," says Professor Allport, "is that people must *expect* war and must prepare for war, before, under war-

[5] Hadley Cantril, Ed., *Tensions That Cause Wars* (Urbana: University of Illinois Press, 1950), pp. 17-18.

minded leadership, they make war. It is in this
sense that 'wars begin in the minds of men.' "[6]

This being so, there can be no "moral equivalent
of war"—that is to say, a harmless outlet for aggression—because men are not endowed with a
fixed reservoir of aggression which can be released
through some "safety valve" and thus expended.
Aggression is rather a habit, which feeds upon itself by building the expectancy that, once tried
successfully, it will solve other problems as well.
"If wars were simply a relief from tension," writes
Professor Allport, "they might conceivably have
their justification. But experience shows that not
only does one war engender another, but it brings
fierce domestic postwar strain and conflict into the
nation itself."[7]

This is precisely what has happened in the twentieth century. Crisis has fed upon crisis and each
conflict has generated the *expectancy* of another.
Meanwhile, the development of nuclear weapons
and rockets has created the technological means
of destroying, or virtually destroying, civilization.
It follows quite obviously that the alteration of
deeply rooted human attitudes, that is to say, the
reshaping of the fatal expectancy of war, is the
foremost requirement of statesmanship in the
twentieth century.

[6] Gordon W. Allport, "The Role of Expectancy," *ibid.*, pp.
43, 48.
[7] *Ibid.*, p .52.

We must generate expectancies of peace as powerful and self-generating as the expectancy of war. We must learn to deal with our adversaries in terms of the *needs* and *hopes* of both sides rather than the demands of one side upon the other. We must remove stridency and bad manners from our diplomacy, because the language of the ultimatum is the language of conflict, because there is no way more certain to turn tension into open conflict than to strike at an adversary's pride and self-respect.

We must strive, in the face of unprecedented need, toward unprecedented acts of political creativity. In one direction, we must move toward broadening forms of association more nearly appropriate to the interdependence of the world than the sovereign nation-state—and as we progress toward a broader world community, we must be prepared to encounter more than a few "unthinkable thoughts." In the other direction, we must turn a substantially greater proportion of our collective energies to the welfare of individuals—to the education and employment of our citizens, to creating societies in which the individual is encouraged and assisted in his striving for personal fulfillment.

It is the nation, or more exactly the pervading force of nationalism, that now obstructs our progress in both of these directions. Posing barriers between communities and exacting heavy sacrifices from its citizens to pursue the quarrels which these barriers engender, the sovereign nation itself is the most pervasive of the old myths that blind us to the realities of our time. Only when we have broken out of the constraints of nationalist mythology will the way be open to the only possible security in the nuclear age—the security of an international community in which men will be free of the terror of the bomb and free at last to pursue the satisfactions of personal fulfillment in civilized societies. We must broaden the frontiers of our loyalties, never forgetting as we do so that it is the human individual, and not the state or any other community, in whom ultimate sovereignty is vested.

J. WILLIAM FULBRIGHT, *Democratic Senator from Arkansas, and Chairman of the Senate Foreign Relations Committee, was born at Sumner, Missouri, on April 9, 1905. He attended Fayetteville, Arkansas, public schools and at the age of twenty graduated from the University of Arkansas with a B. A. in liberal arts. He went to Pembroke College, Oxford University, in England as a Rhodes Scholar and was awarded his B. A. in history in 1928 and his M. A. in 1931. (He was awarded an honorary doctorate degree from Oxford in 1959.) He returned to the United States and studied law at George Washington University, receiving his LL.B. with distinction in 1934.*

In 1935 Mr. Fulbright became a lecturer-in-law at George Washington University. He returned to the University of Arkansas as a member of the law school faculty in 1936 and in 1939 was appointed President of the University. Two years later he was ousted from the presidency for political reasons and as a result of criticism directed at the Governor's policies by a newspaper owned by the Fulbright family. In 1942 he was elected to Congress and became a member of the House Foreign Affairs Committee, where he introduced the "Fulbright Resolution," calling for the participation by the United States in an international organization to maintain peace and generally considered the forerunner to the establishment of the United Nations.

Senator Fulbright is now serving his fourth term in the Senate. He first ran as a candidate for the Senate in 1944, defeating the Governor who had removed him from the University. In 1946 he sponsored the international educational exchange program that bears his name. In 1954 Senator Fulbright was the one member of the Senate to vote against additional funds for the Special Investigating Subcommittee headed by the late Senator Joseph McCarthy, and was a co-sponsor of the censure resolution passed by the Senate against Senator McCarthy. During the same year he was appointed by the President as a member of the United States Delegation to the General Assembly of the United Nations. Chairman of the Banking and Currency Committee from 1955 to 1959, he resigned that post to become Chairman of the Senate Committee on Foreign Relations. He is also a member of the Finance Committee and the Joint Economic Committee.

Senator Fulbright's home is at Fayetteville, Arkansas. He is married to the former Elizabeth Kramer Williams and has two daughters, Mrs. John Winnacker (Elizabeth) and Mrs. Edward Thaddeus Foote II (Roberta).